GÖTZ von BERLICHINGEN

JOHANN WOLFGANG von GOETHE

GÖTZ
von BERLICHINGEN

A Play

Translated by
CHARLES E. PASSAGE
Associate Professor of Comparative Literature
Brooklyn College of The City University of New York

FREDERICK UNGAR PUBLISHING CO.
NEW YORK

Second Printing, 1976

Copyright© 1965 by Frederick Ungar Publishing Co., Inc.

Printed in the United States of America

ISBN 0-8044-6187-2

Library of Congress Catalog Card No. 65-16623

INTRODUCTION

As the Middle Ages were drawing to their close in central Europe, major economic and social changes were operating to the advantage of the high nobility and of the free cities but to the decided disadvantage of the lower nobility and of the peasantry. The latter groups felt themselves aggrieved, and their grievances found expression in local feuds and wars. By rights their cause should have received support from the Emperor, whose subjects they were without intermediary, but often enough the Emperor found his own powers undercut by the princes and by impersonal factors beyond anyone's control. The fact of the matter was that a mysterious and far-reaching change was shifting all the components of society inexorably out of old chivalric patterns and into new patterns, and some people were getting hurt in the process.

Most seriously affected of the lower nobility were the free knights (Reichsritter), whose ancestors in the glorious age before and after 1200 had been the military mainstay of the Emperors in time of war and patrons of the arts in time of peace. Now they were an anomaly and without function. Mercenaries had supplanted them in warfare, and the arts had fled before the boorish manners of their old castles. Here and there was a knight who clung to the ancient better ways, and two such, Gottfried von Berlichingen and Franz von Sickingen, were proud youths of fifteen and fourteen respectively when they attended the Diet convoked by Emperor Maximilian in Worms in 1495 to deal with these grave problems. It was the accomplishment of the Diet to promulgate the "Permanent Peace" (der ewige Landfriede) which abolished the time-honored practice of private warfare among knights (das Faustrecht) as a means of settling disputes; henceforth disputes were to be submitted to the new Imperial Court (das Reichskammergericht), which would dispense justice on the basis of Roman Law. The results of the new judicial order were less than perfect, and the economics of the age resisted legislation.

The free knights found as often as not that their Emperor was remote and busy, that a high prince commanded more influence than they did, and that urban commerce paid better than their own meagre agriculture. To press their peasant tenants was to drive them to revolt or to mercenary service, where a sturdy peasant was the equal of a knight. In this dilemma a knight could choose to sell himself out to army leaders, or to mercantile interests, or to some powerful prince—or he could become a plundering highwayman. Not a few chose the latter alternative, with the result that many a castle became an out-and-out robber's nest. Legally untouchable, those fortified structures controlled roads that merchants were obliged to travel and offered points of safety for those who harassed their slow convoys. The mercantile cities feared and hated those dangerous walls and towers; ambitious princes coveted the lands around them. Their independence was visibly doomed.

Some forty miles east of Heidelberg there was situated on the Jaxt, a small tributary stream of the Neckar, the castle of Jaxthausen, where Gottfried (or Götz) von Berlichingen was born in 1480. His life, which was almost exactly parallel in time to the lives of Martin Luther and Dr. Faustus, followed, unlike theirs, the conventional pattern of the knightly class. Delighting in military sport as a child, and averse to books, he spent the years from age fourteen to age seventeen (1494-1497) as a page in service to his cousin, Konrad von Berlichingen. Upon the latter's death he took service with Frederick IV, Margrave of Brandenburg-Ansbach, achieving knighthood and a reputation as a redoubtable warrior. In one battle he lost his right hand, which was replaced by the famous "iron hand" for which he was thereafter known, a "sort of glove into which the arm-stump was fitted and made fast." Through the first two decades of the sixteenth century he was almost continuously engaged in those private wars—"honorable feuds," as they were called—which had presumably been abolished by the "Permanent Peace" of 1495. In addition to fifteen such which he prosecuted in his own interests, Götz was more than once selected by belligerent parties to lead expeditions in the interests of others. His merchant-convoy plunderings directed against the city of Nürnberg and his campaigns against the princely Bishop of Bamberg in 1512-1513 resulted in his being declared an outlaw of the Empire, and only after considerable difficulty did he buy his way free in 1514. In 1519 he supported the Duke of Württemberg in a larger-scale war against the Swabian League (der schwäbische Bund), an alliance of princes and cities, and in that same year he was besieged in Möckmühl Castle on the Jaxt. When supplies and ammunition ran out he surrendered on condition that he and his troops be allowed to go their ways freely. The terms were accepted by the besiegers, who promptly arrested Götz and his men when they sought to leave the castle. For three and a half years, until October of 1522, they held him prisoner in nearby Heilbronn, whence he finally obtained release through the influence of Franz von Sickingen by paying a heavy fine of 2,000 florins and by taking an oath to renounce feuding forever. For a couple of years he bided by his promise, but during the peasant revolt of 1525 he was forced, so he relates, to assume leadership of a contingent of peasant forces. He bargained for and obtained a four-week term of this leadership, and when the term was up he withdrew as he had specified. To his enemies, however, four weeks and four years were all the same. When the uprising was put down they brought him to trial in Speyer in 1526, and when he was acquitted there the League reinstated charges against him in Augsburg in 1528. This time he was found guilty, spent the two years until 1530 in prison, and obtained release only by taking a new oath which bound him never to spend a night outside his own castle and never to mount a horse. On these terms he lived for ten years until Emperor Charles V absolved him from his promise in order to enlist him in a campaign against the Turks. After brave service against the Turks in 1542 and against the French in 1544 he retired to his castle of Hornberg and spent his final peaceful years in the composition of his autobiography. He was twice married—both wives having the name of Dorothea—and had seven sons and three daughters.

* * * *

It was a sturdy, handsome, self-confident sixteen-year-old

Goethe who had left his native Frankfurt-on-the-Main in 1765 to travel eastward across Germany and enroll for studies in the fashionable and Francophile University of Leipzig. It was a curiously distressed youth who came home again in September of 1768, just after his nineteenth birthday, in an invalid state. The precise nature of the illness is unknown, but it was as much spiritual as physical, and it was serious. Slow convalescence occupied the next eighteen or nineteen months and it was attended by a kind of Christian mystical experience that contrasted sharply with the debonaire existence of his three years away at school. With the return of health in the spring of 1770 came a return of naturally robust spirits, and therewith a new phase of the young man's personality rose to the ascendant. This was to be his "Storm and Stress" phase, which would produce the literary works that astounded his generation and launch his European fame. It was to end in the latter months of 1775 to make way for a new and antithetical phase, that of the so-called Classical author and man who served the Duke of Weimar.

It was apparently about the time of his restoration to health in the spring of 1770 that he first read the *Life History of Sir Götz of Berlichingen* (Lebensbeschreibung des Herrn Gözens von Berlichingen) in the version published in Nürnberg in 1731. A vivid impression of the sixteenth-century knight was already in his mind, therefore, when in early April he set out for the University of Strasbourg to study for a degree in law. It cannot have been too long thereafter that he conceived the idea of transposing the work into dramatic form. Recalling this youthful period of his life many years later in his autobiography, Goethe wrote:

> I concealed from him [his new friend Herder] most carefully the interest I had in certain subjects which had taken deep root in my mind and which were striving gradually to develop into poetic forms. They were Götz von Berlichingen and Faust. The figure of a rough, well-meaning, independent man in a wild and lawless age aroused my deep interest. . . . Now I carried these, like many other

subjects, in my mind, thought them over with delight in my
solitary hours, without, however, writing anything down.

The months in Strasbourg from April, 1770, to August, 1771,
which closed with his return home on the day preceding his twenty-second birthday, were full of vital, formative experiences. The
law degree was taken in due course, but that was incidental. Far
more meaningful for the human and artistic development of the
young man was the poignant romance with the Alsatian pastor's
daughter Friederike Brion in the rural hamlet of Sesenheim. Dis-
guised as a poor theological student, he had first come upon her
in the autumn of 1770, and a profound affection quickly flowered
in both their hearts. Lyrical happiness gladdened the horseback
rides down from Strasbourg, as some of the poet's most winsome
verses attest. Bitter sorrow marked their final farewells in the summer of 1771. There were, no doubt, compelling practical reasons
for the break-up. Goethe was a young man of immense poten-
tialities; he was aware of the fact; Friederike was a simple girl
whose life was cast in simple patterns of domestic ways. They
were, in short, incompatible. All the same, a profound sense of
guilt haunted the departing lover. The Maria of the drama, in
so far as she represents Friederike—and the resemblance is far
from total—is the author's tribute to the steadfastly loyal girl who
with dignity lived down a faithless lover's betrayal. The shabby
desertion of Maria by Weislingen is in part the expression of the
author's guilty conscience. A friend of Goethe's forwarded a copy
of the completed play to Friederike, and to this friend Goethe re-
marked in the accompanying letter: "Poor Friederike will be somewhat consoled when the faithless one—i.e. Weislingen—is poisoned."

Even more important among the formative experiences of
Strasbourg was Goethe's friendship with the young philosopher
Herder. Only five years older than the poet, Herder was consid-
erably older in experience and already the author of published
works of distinction. A serious eye defect had brought him to
Strasbourg for an operation by the medical faculty of the uni-

versity. Enforced seclusion in darkened rooms for a period of
months made him accessible to his visitor, who patiently bore with
his irritable nature in order to learn some of his extraordinary
ideas. They spoke of Homer, of the Bible, of English literature;
they spoke of Shakespeare as not only a towering genius but as the
much-needed counterforce to French Classical drama, the imitation of which had swamped German drama in a morass of tedium
and bad rhetoric; they spoke of Voltaire as the evil genius of
art and of the age. They spoke too of matters less directly related
to literature, for Herder's mind roved over a large area of human
affairs, but these specific literary notions were to coalesce in Goethe's mind into a program for his own creative work. Shakespeare
now became the subject of his intense study. From Shakespeare
he deduced dramatic principles wholly opposed to the strict rules
by which Corneille and Racine had determined their art. Henceforth he was to write plays with multiple characters, multiple
scenes, multiple plots, with widely varying vocabulary and style,
with elements of the grotesque placed side by side with elements
of nobility, with representatives of different social classes, and
above all with a maximum of emotional expression. Not the classical rules, but the human heart in its sensitive goodness was to be
the sole arbiter of what was suitable for inclusion in a play. *Götz
von Berlichingen* was the triumphant application of the new
"Shakespeareanizing" method.

Finally, the Strasbourg months provided Goethe with a new
human milieu that was to be immensely important for the de-
termination of his artistic direction. The city was located in
French territory politically, but culturally it was, as it had been
for centuries, the point where German and French ways of life
met in striking contrast. While in Leipzig, far off to the east in
German territory, Goethe had been an eager Francophile; in
Strasbourg now, he readily agreed to his fellow students' proposal to speak only German, and he looked with favor on the
German customs and dress of the local population. The generation was beginning to sense the uniqueness of the national character. An incipient nationalism was in the air. One of Goethe's

young friends is described as one who "might have been set up as a model of German youth." His name was Lerse, and under that name he enters directly into our drama, there to play himself.

Full of new ideas and oriented now by Herder, Goethe returned to his native Frankfurt on August 27, 1771, the eve, as has been mentioned, of his twenty-second birthday. Three months later, a letter dated November 28 informed his Strasbourg friend Salzmann that he was excitedly engaged in a wholly new project:

> My whole genius is given to an undertaking which makes me forget Shakespeare, Homer, everything. I am dramatizing the history of one of the noblest Germans, to rescue the memory of a worthy man.

In six weeks' time he had completed the first version of the play, which bore the title: *History of Gottfried of Berlichingen with the Iron Hand, Dramatized* (Geschichte Gottfriedens von Berlichingen mit der eisernen Hand, dramatisiert). The source work is unquestionably Götz's own autobiography, supplemented by some historical data especially out of Datt's *De pace publica*, as Goethe himself states, but, apart from the hero, the memorable characters are strictly creations of the author's fancy. Weislingen, Franz, Georg, Lerse, and the three women characters, Adelheid, Maria, and Elizabeth, are all without foundation in the source work. Even such historically guaranteed personages as the Bishop of Bamberg and Götz's fellow knights are completely reinterpreted in the drama. In brief, the word "dramatized," as it figures in the title of the play, is a misleading term.

Salzmann received the manuscript before the end of December, 1771, and wrote back enthusiastic praise of it. The copy of the manuscript forwarded to Herder, however, was accompanied by deferential remarks that sought to anticipate adverse comments from his difficult mentor. Months passed with no reply at all, and when the reply did come, it was, Goethe records, "unfriendly and harsh." Humbly the author agreed that Herder was right in saying that "Shakespeare had quite spoiled him" and promised a thoroughgoing revision. The revision was undertaken the following spring. Whole scenes were excised in the interest of central focusing and over-all unity. The role of Adelheid was considerably abridged. Some new scenes were added to tie the action more tightly together. Motivations received sharper definition. The language was made less stilted. The first draft, then laid aside, was published only after the author's death in 1832. It was the second version, entitled now simply *Götz von Berlichingen*, that brought the twenty-three-year-old Goethe instantaneous fame upon its publication in the summer of 1773.

Rarely has a literary work been launched at a more timely moment. Psychologically the public had been prepared over a period of years for precisely this combination of Rousseauistic emotionalism, "Shakespearean" method, glorification of the national past, and confidence in the national character. The public went wild with enthusiasm. The reviewer in the *Teutscher Merkur* designated the play in September of 1773 as "the most beautiful, the most captivating monstrosity," thus pointing up both the charm of the work and its striking irregularity as judged by standards of traditional theatre. Ultra-conservatives probably agreed with Frederick the Great of Prussia, who in 1780 termed it an "imitation détestable de ces mauvaises pièces anglaises," but from the moment of the triumphantly successful première in Berlin on April 12, 1774, the public at large could not get enough of it. Bad imitations were guaranteed a brief hearing if nothing more, and after a spate of these in German—some forty at least—the work inspired a host of foreign imitations. Sir Walter Scott's translation of it in 1799 formed the point of departure for his own historical romances in prose. In combination with Scott's influence and with Schiller's, it gave impetus to a generation of French writers of historical romances in prose or in dramatic form: Victor Hugo, Alexandre Dumas, and others. In Germany it established a genre which Schiller could first adapt to make *Don Carlos* and further adapt to make his serious historical plays from *Wallenstein* onward. As for Goethe himself, *Götz von Berlichingen* transformed him from a writer for a limited circle to a writer of national renown. The following year (1774) *Werther* was to extend his fame throughout Europe, and therewith was laid the foundation for a career of an author of permanent significance for all of Western Civilization.

As for the play itself, time reveals it as less overwhelming than its own generation found it to be. Admittedly it is mannered: the loose construction is too loose; its language has quaintly aged. Its fluid continuum of action, on the other hand, is oddly anticipatory of the moving pictures, while its impressionistic technique seems fresh and modern. Present-day taste finds very appealing these scenes, each separately lighted, that pass into shadow to allow the next lighted scene to emerge. There is a certain durable magic in the process. Time has revealed the emotions of the play to be genuinely human; its characters win our hearts still; a lyric charm and a breath of idealistic youth reach us from across almost two centuries since its composition. It is perennially a more lovable play than many a work with less obvious faults.

GÖTZ von BERLICHINGEN

CHARACTERS

EMPEROR MAXIMILIAN
GÖTZ VON BERLICHINGEN
ELIZABETH, his wife
MARIA, his sister
KARL, his little son
GEORG, his page
THE BISHOP OF BAMBERG
WEISLINGEN
ADELHEID VON WALLDORF } at the Bishop's court
LIEBETRAUT
THE ABBOT OF FULDA
OLEARIUS, Doctor of both kinds of law
BROTHER MARTIN
HANS VON SELBITZ
FRANZ VON SICKINGEN
LERSE
FRANZ, Weislingen's page
Ladies-in-waiting to Adelheid
METZLER
SIEVERS
LINK } leaders of the rebellious peasants
KOHL
WILD
Lords and ladies of the Bamberg court
Imperial Councilors
Aldermen of Heilbronn
Judges of the secret tribunal

Two Nürnberg merchants
MAX STUMPF, a server of the Count Palatine
A stranger   ⎫
The bride's father ⎬ peasants
The bridegroom   ⎭
Horsemen of the Berlichingen, Weislingen, and Bamberg forces
A Captain, officers, and soldiers of the Imperial army
An innkeeper
The Court Summoner
Citizens of Heilbronn
The city watchman
The jailer
Peasants
A gypsy leader
Gypsies and gypsywomen

Time: An indeterminate period of years around 1520.
Place: Various localities in southwestern Germany.

ACT I

[SCENE 1]

Schwarzenberg in Franconia. An inn.
Metzler and Sievers at table. Two mounted soldiers by the fire.
The innkeeper.

SIEVERS: Hänsel, another glass of brandy, and be Christian about the measure.

INNKEEPER: You never get enough.

METZLER *(in a low voice to Sievers)*: Tell that again about Berlichingen. Those Bambergers there are so mad they're just about purple.

SIEVERS: Bambergers? What are *they* doing here?

METZLER: Weislingen has been up at the castle for two days now with the Count; they were his escort. I don't know where he came from. They're waiting for him. He's going back to Bamberg.

SIEVERS: Who is this Weislingen?

METZLER: The Bishop's right-hand man, a powerful nobleman who is laying for Götz.

SIEVERS: He'd better watch out.

METZLER *(softly)*: Keep it up! *(Aloud)* Since when has Götz been having trouble again with the Bishop of Bamberg? Rumor had it that everything was settled and smoothed over.

SIEVERS: Yes, *you* settle something with priests! When the Bishop saw he wasn't getting anywhere and kept getting the short end, he came crawling for mercy and was anxious to get a settlement arranged. And loyal-hearted Berlichingen gave in, unbelievably, the way he always does when he has the upper hand.

METZLER: God shield him! An upright gentleman.

5

SIEVERS: Just think, isn't it a shame? There they pick off a page of his when it's the last thing he's expecting. But he'll fix them again for that!

METZLER: It's a dirty shame, though, that his last trick didn't come off. He must have been fit to be tied.

SIEVERS: I don't think that a thing like that got him down for long. Remember too that everything was reconnoitered down to the last detail—when the Bishop would be leaving the watering place, how many horsemen he had with him, which road he was traveling. And if things hadn't been betrayed by treacherous people he would have blessed that bath for him and rubbed him down besides.

FIRST SOLDIER: Why are you discussing our Bishop? I think you're looking for trouble.

SIEVER: Mind your own affairs! You've got no business at our table.

SECOND SOLDIER: Who told you to talk disrespectfully about our Bishop?

SIEVERS: Do I have to answer to you? Look at the monkey!

FIRST SOLDIER *(boxes his ears.)*

METZLER: Kill the bastard!

(They start a fight.)

SECOND SOLDIER: Come on over here if you've got the guts!

INNKEEPER *(parting them by force)*: Quiet down! Damnation! Go on outside if you've got something to settle between you! In my barroom I want things decent and orderly. *(He shoves the soldiers out the door.)* And you two donkeys, what are you trying to start?

METZLER: Don't let your tongue run away with you, Hänsel, or we'll be after your bald head. Come on, friend, we'll beat 'em up outside.

(Enter two outriders of Berlichingen's.)

FIRST OUTRIDER: What's going on?

SIEVERS: Hey! Good day to you, Peter! Good day, Veit! Where do you come from?

SECOND OUTRIDER: Don't you dare let on who it is we serve.

SIEVERS *(softly)*: Then your master Götz can't be too far off?

FIRST OUTRIDER: Shut up!—Got trouble?

SIEVERS: You ran into those fellows outside. They're Bambergers.

FIRST OUTRIDER: What are *they* doing here?

METZLER: Weislingen is up at the castle with His Grace; they were his escort.

FIRST OUTRIDER: Weislingen?

SECOND OUTRIDER *(softly)*: Peter! This is a windfall! *(Aloud)* How long has he been there?

METZLER: Two days now. But he means to leave today, I heard one of those fellows say.

FIRST OUTRIDER *(softly)*: Didn't I tell you he came this way? We could have watched a good long while over there. Come on, Veit.

SIEVERS: Help us beat up those Bambergers first.

SECOND OUTRIDER: There are two of *you*. We've got to get going. See you later!

(The outriders leave.)

SIEVERS: Stinkers! Those outriders! If you don't pay them they won't lift a finger.

METZLER: I'd swear they're on a mission. Whose employ are they in?

SIEVERS: I ain't supposed to say.—They're in service with Götz.

METZLER: Is that so!—Now let's get after those two outside. Come on! As long as I've got a club I'm not afraid of their oven-spits.

SIEVERS: If we could just once go after those princes this way, that are peeling the hides right off of us!

*

[SCENE 2]

A lodge in the forest.

GÖTZ *(beneath the linden tree in front of the door)*: What's keeping my outriders? I have to keep walking back and forth or sleep will overtake me. Five days and nights now on the lookout. It sours the little life and freedom a man has. All the same, when I get you, Weislingen, I'll call it a good job done. *(He starts to pour from the bottle.)* Empty again! Georg!—As long as there's no lack of this and of good courage I can laugh at princes' schemes and greed for power.—Georg!—Send your toady Weislingen around to your kith and kin, have him blacken my name. Go to it. I've got my eyes open. You got away from me, Bishop! So your precious Weislingen can pay the score. —Georg! Can't the lad hear? Georg! Georg!

THE PAGE *(in grown man's armor)*: Sir?

GÖTZ: Where have you been? Sleeping? What the devil kind of mummery is this? Come here! You look all right! Don't be bashful, lad. You're fine! If you could just fill it out! Is that Hans's armor?

GEORG: He wanted to take a bit of a nap and he unbuckled it.

GÖTZ: It's more comfortable than its master.

GEORG: Don't be angry. I took it away quietly and put it on, and took my father's old sword down off the wall, ran out into the yard, and drew it.

GÖTZ: And hacked about with it? That must have helped the bushes and thorns. Is Hans asleep?

GEORG: At your call he jumped up and bellowed to me that you were calling. I was trying to unbuckle the armor when I heard you the second and third times.

GÖTZ: Go and give him back his armor and tell him to be ready and to look after the horses.

GEORG: Oh, I fed them all right and put the bridles back on. You can ride whenever you're ready.

GÖTZ: Bring me a jug of wine. Give Hans a glass too. Tell him to be alert; he'll need to be. I hope any minute now my scouts will be coming back.

GEORG: Oh, Sir!

GÖTZ: What's the matter?

GEORG: Can't I go along?

GÖTZ: Some other time, Georg, when we capture some merchants and get their carts.

GEORG: Some other time! You have said that so often. O, this time, this time! I only want to run along behind, hide off to one side. I'll gather up your spent arrows for you.

GÖTZ: The next time, Georg. First you'll have to have a doublet, a helmet, and a spear.

GEORG: Take me along. If I had been along the last time you wouldn't have lost your cross-bow.

GÖTZ: You know about that?

GEORG: You threw it at the enemy's head and one of the foot soldiers picked it up, and there it was, gone. I know, don't I?

GÖTZ: Did my men tell you about this?

GEORG: Of course. And in return I whistle all kinds of tunes for them while we curry the horses, and teach them all sorts of jolly songs.

GÖTZ: You're a brave lad.

GEORG: Take me along so I can prove it.

GÖTZ: The next time, on my word. Unarmed as you are, you mustn't go into battle. The times to come will need men too. I tell you, boy, it will be a sweet time: princes will offer their treasures for a man that they now hate. So, Georg, give Hans back his armor and bring me some wine.

(Exit Georg.)

What is keeping my men? I can't understand it.—A monk! Now where is he coming from?

(Enter Brother Martin.)

Reverend Father, good evening! Where are you coming from so late? Man of holy peace, you put many a knight to shame.

MARTIN: I thank you, noble Sir. And for the time being I'm only a humble Brother when it comes to titles. Augustin is my name in religion, but I like best to hear Martin, my baptismal name.[1]

GÖTZ: You are tired, Brother Martin, and doubtless thirsty.

(Enter the page.)

Here comes some wine just at the right time.

MARTIN: A drink of water for me. I am not permitted to drink wine.

GÖTZ: Is that a vow?

MARTIN: No, gracious Sir, it is not against my vow to drink wine; but because wine is against my vow, I drink no wine.

GÖTZ: How do you mean that?

MARTIN: It is well for you that you do not understand it. Eating and drinking, I believe, are the life of man.

GÖTZ: True.

MARTIN: When you have eaten and drunk, you are as new born, you are stronger, more courageous, more fit for your work. Wine rejoices the heart of man, and joy is the mother of all virtues. When you have drunk wine you are everything twice over that you are supposed to be. You think twice as easily, you are twice as enterprising, twice as quick at execution.

GÖTZ: The way I drink it, that is true.

MARTIN: That is what I am talking about too. But we . . .

---

[1]Martin Luther was an Augustinian monk at Erfurt, but the present character seems to be an independent personage intended, apparently, only to suggest the *era* of the actual Luther.

(Enter Georg with water.)

Götz *(aside to Georg)*: Go down to the Dachsbach road and put
your ear to the ground and see if you don't hear horses coming.
Then come straight back here.

MARTIN: . . . but we, when we have eaten and drunk, are precisely the opposite of what we are supposed to be. Our sleepy
digestion attunes the head to the belly, and in the weakness
of an over-copious repose desires are engendered which quickly
grow higher than their mother's head.

Götz: One glass, Brother Martin, won't disturb your sleep. You
have done a lot of walking today.

(He raises a toast to him.)

All fighters!

MARTIN: In God's name! *(They clink glasses.)*
I cannot endure idle people. And yet I cannot say that all
monks are idle; they do what they can. I have just come from
St. Vitus', where I slept last night. The prior took me out
into the garden; that is their beehive, you know. Excellent
lettuce! Cabbage to warm your heart! Especially cauliflower
and artichokes, like none in Europe!

Götz: But that, of course, isn't your province.

(He gets up, looks for the boy, and returns.)

MARTIN: Would that God had made me a gardener or a worker
in the laboratory! Then I could be happy. My abbot is fond
of me—my monastery in Erfurt in Saxony—and he knows I
cannot be still. So he sends me around wherever there is something to be looked after. I am on my way to the Bishop of
Constance.

Götz: Another one! Successful discharge of your business!

MARTIN: The same to you.

Götz: Why do you look at me that way, Brother?

Martin: Because I am in love with your armor.

Götz: You would like some like it? It is heavy and burdensome to wear.

Martin: What is not burdensome in this world? And nothing seems more burdensome to me than not to be allowed to be a human being. Poverty, chastity, and obedience—three vows, each one of which separately seems the most unbearable thing to Nature, and they are all three unbearable. And to pant meekly all one's life beneath this weight or beneath the far more oppressive burden of conscience! O Sir, what are the tribulations of your life compared to the miseries of a class which, out of misunderstood desire to get nearer to God, condemns the best impulses by which we exist and grow and thrive?

Götz: If your vow were not so sacred, I should like to persuade you to put on a suit of armor. I'd give you a horse and we would set off together.

Martin: Would to God that my shoulders had the strength to bear the armor and my arm the power to thrust an enemy off his horse!—Poor weak hand that has never been accustomed to wielding anything but crucifixes and banners of peace or swinging anything but censers, how would you manage lance and sword! My voice, tuned solely to Aves and Hallelujahs, would herald my weakness to the enemy, while yours would overwhelm him. No vow would keep me from entering again the Order which my Creator Himself founded.

Götz: Prosperous return journey!

Martin: To that I shall drink only for you. Return to my cage will be unhappy in any case. When you, Sir, return inside your walls with the consciousness of your bravery and strength which no weariness can affect, and for the first time after a long interval stretch out unarmed on your bed, safe from enemy at-

tack, and relax in sleep that tastes sweeter to you than drink
tastes to me after a long thirst—then you can talk about happiness.

Götz: On the other hand, that occurs only rarely.

Martin (more ardently): And when it does come, it is a fore-
taste of heaven.—When you return laden with booty from your
enemies and recall: this one I knocked off his horse before he
could shoot, and that one I ran down horse and all—and then
you ride up to your castle, and . . .

Götz: What are you thinking?

Martin: And your women folk! (He pours himself a drink.) To
the health of your wife! (He wipes his eyes.) You do have one?

Götz: A noble and excellent woman.

Martin: Blessed is the man who hath a virtuous wife, for the
numbers of his days shall be double.[1] I know no women, yet
woman was the crown of creation.

Götz (to himself): I feel sorry for him. The feeling of his class
is eating his heart out.

Georg (running in): Sir, I hear horses at a gallop. Two of them.
It is surely they.

Götz: Lead out my horse. Hans shall ride. Farewell, dear Brother,
God be with you. Have courage and patience. God will make
room for you.[2]

Martin: May I ask your name?

Götz: Forgive me. Farewell. (He extends his left hand to him.)

Martin: Why do you give me only your left hand? Am I not
worthy of the knightly right one?

Götz: Even if you were the Emperor, you would have to be
content with this one. My right one, although not useless in
warfare, is insensitive to the pressure of love. It is identical
with its glove. You see: it is made of iron.

---

[1]Ecclesiasticus 26:1.
[2]Genesis 26:22.

MARTIN: Then you are Götz von Berlichingen! O God, I thank Thee that Thou hast caused me to behold him, this man whom the princes hate and to whom the oppressed turn.

(He takes his right hand.)

Give me this hand, let me kiss it.

GÖTZ: That you shall not.

MARTIN: Let me do so! Thou, more precious than a reliquary hand through which the holiest blood has flowed, lifeless instrument animated by the noblest spirit's reliance upon God!

GÖTZ *(puts on his helmet and takes up his lance.)*

MARTIN: There was a monk of ours some time ago who visited you when it was shot off before the walls of Landshut. The way he told us about what you suffered and how greatly it pained you to be maimed in your profession, and how you recalled having heard about someone who had only one hand and yet served for a long time as a brave cavalier—I shall never forget it.

(Enter the two outriders.)

GÖTZ *(goes over to them; they speak in secret.)*

MARTIN *(continues speaking meanwhile)*: I shall never forget how he spoke in the simplest and noblest confidence in God: Even if I had twelve hands and Thy grace availed me not, what would they avail? Thus with one I can . . .

GÖTZ: To Haslach Forest then. *(He turns to Martin.)* Farewell. worthy Brother Martin. *(He kisses him.)*

MARTIN: Do not forget me! I shall not forget you!

(Exit Götz.)

How choked my heart became when I saw him! He said nothing, and yet my spirit was able to discern his. It is a delight to see a great man.

GEORG: Reverend Sir, will you sleep in our house?

MARTIN: Can I get a bed?

GEORG: No, Sir. I know about beds only from hearsay. At our lodge there is nothing but straw.

MARTIN: It will do. What is your name?

GEORG: Georg, reverend Sir.

MARTIN: Georg! There you have a brave patron saint.

GEORG: They say he was a horseman. That's what I want to be.

MARTIN: Wait a moment. *(He takes out a prayerbook and gives the lad a holy card.)* There you have him. Follow his example, be brave and fear God. *(Exit Martin.)*

GEORG: Oh, a beautiful white horse! If only I had one like that! —And the golden armor!—That's a nasty dragon.—I only shoot sparrows now.—Saint George, make me tall and strong, give me a lance like this one, and armor, and a horse. Then let me find the dragons!

*

[SCENE 3]

Jaxthausen. Götz's castle.
Elizabeth. Maria. Karl, his little son.

KARL: Please, Auntie dear, tell me again about the Worthy Child. That's such a nice story.

MARIA: You tell it to me, you little rogue. Then I will hear whether you pay attention.

KARL: Wait a bit, I want to think.—*Once upon a time* . . . yes: *Once upon a time there was a child and his mother was ill. Then the child went* . . .

MARIA: No, no. *Then his mother said, "Dear child* . . .

KARL: *I am ill* . . .

MARIA: *. . . and cannot go out."* . . .

KARL: *And she gave him money and said, "Go find yourself a breakfast." Along came a poor man . . .*

MARIA: *The child set out. And he came upon an old man who was* . . . Well, Karl?

KARL: *Who was . . . old . . .*

MARIA: That's right! *. . . who could scarcely walk any more, and he said, "Dear child, . . .*

KARL: *. . . give me something. I ate no bread yesterday nor yet today." Then the child gave him the money . . .*

MARIA: *. . . which was to have been for his breakfast.*

KARL: *Then the old man said . . .*

MARIA: *Then the old man took the child . . .*

KARL: *. . . by the hand and said . . . and he was seen to be a beautiful and radiant saint, and said, . . . "Dear child, . . .*

MARIA: *. . . for your charity Our Blessed Lady will reward you through me: What sick person soever you touch . . .*

KARL: *. . . with your hand"* . . . It was the right hand, I think . . .

MARIA: Yes.

KARL: *". . . he shall be made well."*

MARIA: *Then the child ran home and was unable to speak for joy . . .*

KARL: *. . . and fell upon his mother's neck and wept for joy.*

MARIA: *Then his mother cried out, "What thing is happening to me!" and was* . . . Well, Karl?

KARL: *. . . and was . . . and was . . .*

MARIA: But you're not paying attention! *. . . and was well. And the child cured king and emperor and became so rich that he built a great monastery.*

ELIZABETH: I cannot understand where my lord stays. It is already five days and nights that he has been away, and he hoped to carry out his exploit so soon.

MARIA: It has long worried me. If I had such a husband who

was forever exposing himself to dangers, I would die in the first year.

ELIZABETH: I, on the contrary, thank God for having made me of sterner stuff.

KARL: But must Father ride out if it's so dangerous?

MARIA: It is his will to do so.

ELIZABETH: Of course he must, Karl dear.

KARL: Why?

ELIZABETH: Do you remember how the last time he rode out he brought back rolls for you?

KARL: Will he bring me some more?

ELIZABETH: I think so. You see, there was a tailor from Stuttgart, and he was a splendid archer and had won first place in the shooting match at Cologne.

KARL: Was it a lot?

ELIZABETH: A hundred thalers. And afterwards they wouldn't give it to him.

MARIA: That was mean, wasn't it, Karl?

KARL: Mean people!

ELIZABETH: Then the tailor came to your father and asked him if he would help him get his money. And so he rode out and carried off a couple of merchants of the people in Cologne and kept bothering them until they came across with the money. Wouldn't you have ridden out too?

KARL: No! I would have to go through a deep, deep forest, and there are gypsies and witches in it.

ELIZABETH: A fine fellow you are, afraid of witches.

MARIA: You will do better, Karl, just to live in your castle as a good and Christian knight. There is opportunity enough for good deeds right in one's own lands. The most upright knights do more injustice than justice on their expeditions.

ELIZABETH: Sister, you don't know what you're saying. God grant that our boy shall grow braver with time and that he won't take after this Weislingen who has dealt so faithlessly with my husband.

MARIA: Let us not pass judgment, Elizabeth. My brother is very bitter, and you are too. I am more of a spectator in the whole matter and I can be more fair.

ELIZABETH: There is no excuse for him.

MARIA: What I have heard about him fascinates me. How many kind and good things your husband himself used to tell about him! How happy their boyhood was when they were pages of the Margrave together.

ELIZABETH: That may well be. But tell me, what good can there ever have been in a man who lays snares for his best and truest friend, sells his services to my husband's enemies, and tries to deceive our excellent Emperor, who is so gracious to us, by false and malicious representations!

KARL: There's Father! There's Father! The tower warder is blowing his call. Hey there, open the gate!

ELIZABETH: Here he comes with booty.

(*Enter an outrider.*)

OUTRIDER: We've been hunting and we've made a catch! God greet you, noble ladies!

ELIZABETH: Have you caught Weislingen?

OUTRIDER: Him and three horsemen.

ELIZABETH: What happened that kept you away so long?

OUTRIDER: We were lying in wait for him between Nürnberg and Bamberg but he just wouldn't come along; and yet we knew he was on his way. Finally we got on his trail. He had taken a side road and was sitting comfortably with the Count at Schwarzenberg.

ELIZABETH: They would like to make him too an enemy of my husband's.

OUTRIDER: That's just what I said right away to the master. Off he went, and rode into Haslach Forest. And then something curious happened. As we are riding along in the darkness, there happened to be a shepherd guarding his flocks right there and five wolves are attacking the flock and going stoutly to it. Then our master laughed and said, "Good luck, my hearties, good luck everywhere and to us as well!" And we were all cheered by the good omen. And meanwhile Weislingen comes riding along with four squires.

MARIA: My heart trembles within me.

OUTRIDER: I and my comrade, as the master had commanded, crept up close to him as if we had grown together so that he couldn't stir or budge, and the master and Hans attacked the squires and took them prisoners. One of them got away.

ELIZABETH: I am curious to see him. Are they coming soon?

OUTRIDER: They're riding up the valley. They will be here in a quarter of an hour.

MARIA: He must be downcast.

OUTRIDER: He looks grim enough.

MARIA: The sight of him will pain my heart.

ELIZABETH: Ah!—I will get supper ready at once. You must all be hungry.

OUTRIDER: Thoroughly.

ELIZABETH: Take the key to the cellar and fetch some of the best wine. They've earned it.

(Exit Elizabeth.)

KARL: I'll come with you, Auntie.

MARIA: Come, boy.

(Exeunt Maria and Karl.)

OUTRIDER: He won't be like his father, or he'd have gone to the stable.

(Enter Götz, Weislingen, and squires.)

GÖTZ *(laying his helmet and sword on the table)*: Unbuckle my armor for me and give me my jerkin. The comfort will feel good. Brother Martin, you were right . . . You gave us a run for our money, Weislingen.

WEISLINGEN *(does not reply, paces back and forth.)*

GÖTZ: Cheer up. Come, lay aside your arms. Where are your clothes? I hope none of them has got lost. *(to the outrider)* Ask his squires and open up the baggage, and take care that nothing goes astray. I could lend you some of mine, too.

WEISLINGEN: Leave me as I am, it makes no difference.

GÖTZ: I could give you a nice clean coat. It's only linen, of course. It's gotten too tight for me. I wore it to the wedding of my gracious lord the Count Palatine, on just the occasion when your Bishop waxed so poisonous about me. Two weeks before that I had captured two of his ships on the Main. And I'm just going up the steps with Franz von Sickingen in the Stag Inn in Heidelberg. Before you get all the way up there is a landing with an iron railing. There stood the Bishop and gave his hand to Franz as he passed and gave it to me too when I came along behind. I laughed to myself and walked over to the Landgrave of Hanau, who has been a very loving gentleman to me, and said, "The Bishop gave me his hand. I'll bet he didn't recognize me." The Bishop heard that, because I talked loud on purpose, and came over defiantly to us and said, "I did indeed give you my hand because I did not recognize you." Then I said, "Sir, I clearly saw that you didn't recognize me, and here you have your hand back again." Then the popinjay's neck got as red as a lobster with anger and he ran into the room to Count Palatine Ludwig and the Prince of Nassau and complained about it. We've had many a good laugh over it ever since.

WEISLINGEN: I wish you would leave me to myself.

GÖTZ: Why? I beg you, be cheerful. You are in my power, and

I won't misuse it.

WEISLINGEN: I wasn't worried on that score. That is your knightly
   duty.

GÖTZ: And you know that it is sacred to me.

WEISLINGEN: I am a captive. Nothing else makes any difference.

GÖTZ: You shouldn't talk that way. What if you had princes to
   deal with and they hung you up by chains in the depths of the
   dungeon and the guard had the task of whistling away your
   sleep?

(Enter the squires with the clothes.)

WEISLINGEN *(takes off garments and puts fresh ones on.)*

(Enter Karl.)

KARL: Good morning, Father.

GÖTZ *(kisses him.)*: Good morning, boy. How have you people
   passed the time here?

KARL: Very cleverly, Father. Auntie says I'm very clever.

GÖTZ: So!

KARL: Did you bring me something?

GÖTZ: Not this time.

KARL: I've learned a lot of things.

GÖTZ: Oh!

KARL: Shall I tell you about the Worthy Child?

GÖTZ: After supper.

KARL: I know something else too.

GÖTZ: What might that be?

KARL: Jaxthausen is a village and castle on the Jaxt. It has belonged for two hundred years to the lords of Berlichingen by
   hereditary right and by right of possession.

GÖTZ: Do you know the Lord of Berlichingen?

KARL *(looks at him fixedly.)*

GÖTZ *(to himself)*: For sheer erudition he doesn't know his own
   father.—To whom does Jaxthausen belong?

KARL: Jaxthausen is a village and castle on the Jaxt.

GÖTZ: I'm not asking you that.—*I* knew every path and road and ford before I knew the names of the river and village and castle.—Is your mother in the kitchen?

KARL: Yes, Father. She's cooking turnips and a roast of lamb.

GÖTZ: You know that too, Little Jack Chef?

KARL: And for dessert Auntie has baked me an apple.

GÖTZ: Can't you eat them raw?

KARL: They taste better this way.

GÖTZ: Always having to have something special.—Weislingen, I'll be right with you. I must see my wife a moment. Come along, Karl.

KARL: Who is the man?

GÖTZ: Speak to him. Tell him to be cheerful.

KARL: There, man, here is my hand. Be cheerful, supper will soon be ready.

WEISLINGEN *(picks him up and kisses him.)*: Fortunate child that knows no evil except supper is delayed. God grant you much joy of the lad, Berlichingen.

GÖTZ: Where there is much light there is also strong shadow— but I would welcome it. We shall see how it turns out.

(Exeunt Götz and Karl.)

WEISLINGEN: Oh, if I could wake up and all this were a dream! In Berlichingen's power, from whom I had hardly worked my way free, whose memory I shunned like fire, whom I hoped to conquer! And he—old, loyal-hearted Götz! Holy God, what will come of all this? Brought back, Adelbert, to the hall where we romped about as boys—when you loved him, hung upon him as on your own soul! Who can come near him and hate him? Oh, I am such a cipher here! Happy times, you are past and gone, when the elder Berlichingen used to sit here by the hearthside and we used to play around him and loved each other as angels love. How worried the Bishop will be, and my friends! I know the whole country will sympathize with my misfortune. But what of that? Can they give me what I am striving for?

Götz *(with a bottle of wine and glasses)*: Till supper is ready we'll have a drink. Come, sit down, make yourself at home. Think of it, you are back with Götz once more. It's a long time since we have eaten together, a long time since we cracked a bottle with each other.

(Raises a toast to him.)

A cheerful heart!

Weislingen: Those times are past.

Götz: God forbid! To be sure, we won't find happier days again than at the Margrave's court when we still shared a bed and went around together. I remember my youth with joy. Do you remember the trouble I got into with that Pole whose curled and pomaded hair I accidentally ruffled with my sleeve?

Weislingen: It was at table, and he lunged at you with a knife.

Götz: I gave him a thorough going over at the time, and later you picked a fight with his friend. We always stuck solidly together as good, stout lads, and everybody acknowledged that of us.

(He pours another glass and offers a toast to Weislingen.)

Castor and Pollux! I always had a good feeling inside me when the Margrave called us that.

Weislingen: It was the Bishop of Würzburg that started it.

Götz: There was a learned gentleman, and yet affable too. I shall never forget him as long as I live, the way he used to pet us, praise our harmony, and always used to call any man fortunate who was his friend's twin brother.

Weislingen: No more of that!

Götz: Why not? I don't know of anything more pleasant after work than to recall the past. In fact, when I think of how we

used to bear joys and sorrows together, used to be everything
to each other, and how I imagined things then, that's the way
it ought to be all our lives. Wasn't that my whole consolation
when this hand of mine was shot off before Landshut and you
nursed me and took more care of me than a brother? I hoped
that Adelbert would be my right hand after that. And now . . .

WEISLINGEN: O!

GÖTZ: If you had followed my advice then, as I urged you to do,
to go with me to Brabant, everything would have continued
to be all right. But that wretched court life kept you back, and
the flirting and dawdling after women. I always told you, if
you took up with those vain and nasty sluts and told them tales
about unsatisfactory marriages, seduced girls, and the harsh
skin of a third party, or whatever else they like to hear about,
you would turn out a scoundrel, as I used to say, Adelbert.

WEISLINGEN: What is all this leading up to?

GÖTZ: I would to God I could forget it or that it were otherwise!
Are you not as free, as nobly born as any man in Germany,
independent, subject only to the Emperor, and you cringe before vassals? What do you get from the Bishop? Because he is
your neighbor and could make trouble for you? Don't you have
arms and friends to trouble him back again? Do you under-
estimate the value of being a free knight who is subject only
to God, his Emperor, and himself! And you go crawling after
the first court lackey of a hoity-toity, envious priest!

WEISLINGEN: Let me speak.

GÖTZ: What have you to say?

WEISLINGEN: You look at princes the way the wolf looks at the
shepherd. And yet, can you blame them for defending the best
interests of their subjects and lands? Are they safe for a minute
from the unjust knights who attack their subjects on every
highway and lay waste their villages and castles? If now, on the
other hand, our beloved Emperor's lands are exposed to the

violence of the archenemy, and he requires aid from the estates, and they can scarcely defend their own lives, is it not a
good spirit that counsels them to think of means of pacifying
Germany, of administering right and justice, so that every man,
great and small, may be allowed to enjoy the blessings of peace?
And you find fault with us, Berlichingen, for entrusting ourselves to their protection when their help is close to us, when
far-off Majesty cannot protect himself?

Götz: Yes, yes, I understand you, Weislingen, if the princes were
the way you describe them we would all have what we want.
Order and peace! I believe it! That's what every bird of prey
wants: to devour its quarry in comfort. Every man's welfare!
If that were the only thing they're getting grey hair over! And
they are toying with our Emperor in a disgraceful fashion. He
means well and would gladly improve matters. Every day along
comes some new tinker with this opinion and that opinion.
And because our master grasps a thing quickly and has but to
speak to set a thousand hands in motion, he thinks everything
will be just that quickly and easily carried out. Then decrees
follow decrees, and one after the other is forgotten. And whatever is grist for the princes' mill, they're right after it and
glory in the order and security of the Empire until they've got
the little fellows under their heels. I'll take my oath that many
a one of them thanks God in his heart that the Turks counter-
balance the Emperor.

Weislingen: You see things from *your* side.

Götz: So does every man. The question is on which side light
and right are, and your movements at least shun the daylight.

Weislingen: You can talk. I am the captive.

Götz: If your conscience is clear, you are free. But how did it
go with the Permanent Peace? I still remember, as a boy of
sixteen I was with the Margrave at the Diet. How the princes
opened their yaps then, and the ecclesiastical ones worst of

all! Your Bishop yowled the Emperor's ear off, as if Justice had become O *so* dear! to his heart. And now he strikes down a page of mine at a time when our quarrels are composed and I don't have a wicked thought. Isn't everything straightened out between us? What business has he got with the lad?

WEISLINGEN: It happened without his knowledge.

GÖTZ: Why doesn't he let him go again?

WEISLINGEN: He hasn't behaved the way he should.

GÖTZ: Not the way he should? By my oath, he has done as he should, as sure as he was captured with your and the Bishop's knowledge. Do you think I was born yesterday, that I am not supposed to see where all this is leading?

WEISLINGEN: You are suspicious and do us an injustice.

GÖTZ: Weislingen, shall I talk to you straight from the shoulder? I am a thorn in your flesh, small as I am, and Sickingen and Selbitz no less so, because we are determined to die before we owe anyone but God for the air we breathe and before we pay loyalty and service to anyone but the Emperor. And now they're stalking me, blackening my reputation with His Majesty and His Majesty's friends and with my neighbors, and spying for some advantage over me. They want me out of the way, no matter what. That's why you took my page prisoner, because you knew I had sent him out to reconnoitre; and he didn't behave as he was supposed to because he didn't betray me to you. And you, Weislingen, are their tool!

WEISLINGEN: Berlichingen!

GÖTZ: Not another word about it! I am a foe of explanations; a man betrays himself or the other fellow, and usually both.

KARL: Come to dinner, Father.

GÖTZ: Good news!—Come! I hope my womenfolk will cheer you up. You used to be a gallant; young ladies had a lot to tell of you. Come!

*

[SCENE 4]

In the episcopal palace at Bamberg. The dining hall.
The Bishop of Bamberg. The Abbot of Fulda. Olearius.
Liebetraut. Courtiers.
At table. Dessert and the great wine cups are being brought in.

THE BISHOP: Are there many of the German nobility now study-
ing at Bologna?

OLEARIUS: Nobles and burghers. And boasting aside, they are
carrying off the highest honors. At the academy there is a saying that goes: "As industrious as a German nobleman." For
though the burghers bring a praiseworthy diligence to bear, in
order to make up through talent for their lack of birth, the
others exert themselves in a praiseworthy competition to en-
hance their inherent dignity by the most splendid accomplish-
ments.

THE ABBOT: Ah!

LIEBETRAUT: What all doesn't a man live to hear! "As industrious
as a German nobleman!" *That* I've never heard in all my days.

OLEARIUS: Yes, they are the admiration of the whole academy. Before long several of the oldest and best skilled of them will be
coming back as *Doctores*. The Emperor will be fortunate in being able to fill the best posts with them.

THE BISHOP: No doubt about it.

THE ABBOT: Do you happen to know, for example, a squire . . . ?
He comes from Hesse . . .

OLEARIUS: There are numbers of Hessians there.

THE ABBOT: His name is . . . It's . . . Don't any of you know? . . .
His mother was a von . . . Oh! His Father had only one eye . . .
and he was a Marshal.

LIEBETRAUT: Von Wildenholz?

THE ABBOT: That's it. Von Wildenholz.

OLEARIUS: I know him well. A young gentleman of many capacities. He is especially renowned for his strength in debate.

THE ABBOT: He gets that from his mother.

LIEBETRAUT: Only her husband failed to praise that in her.

THE BISHOP: What did you say was that Emperor's name that wrote your *Corpus Juris?*

OLEARIUS: Justinian.

THE BISHOP: An excellent gentleman! Long may he live!

OLEARIUS: His memory!

(They drink.)

THE ABBOT: It must be a wonderful book.

OLEARIUS: You might call it the book of all books, a collection of laws, with the sentence ready for any case. And whatever is missing or obscure is supplied by the glosses with which the most learned men have adorned the supremely excellent work.

THE ABBOT: A collection of all laws! Thunderation! Then the Ten Commandments must be in it too.

OLEARIUS: *Implicite* to be sure, though not *explicite.*

THE ABBOT: That's what I mean, just put down without further explication.

THE BISHOP: And the best part of it all is, that, as you say, a state could live in the securest tranquillity and peace wherever it was fully introduced and properly administered.

OLEARIUS: Unquestionably.

THE BISHOP: All Doctors of Law!

OLEARIUS: To that I will drink with enthusiasm.

(They drink.)

Would God that people spoke that way in my homeland!

THE ABBOT: Where are you from, learned Sir?

OLEARIUS: From Frankfurt-on-the-Main, so please Your Eminence.

THE BISHOP: Aren't you gentlemen well thought of there? How does that happen?

OLEARIUS: Oddly enough. I was there to collect my inheritance from my father. The mob all but stoned me when they heard I was a lawyer.

THE ABBOT: God forbid!

OLEARIUS: But the reason for that is this: the Court of Sheriffs, which is held far and wide in great esteem, consists solely of men who are not acquainted with Roman Law. They think it is sufficient to acquire through age and experience a precise knowledge of the internal and the external condition of the city. Thus the citizens and the adjacent areas are ordered in accordance with ancient tradition and a few statutes.

THE ABBOT: Well, that's good.

OLEARIUS: But nowhere near sufficient. Human life is short, and not all cases turn up in one generation. Our book of laws is a collection of such cases over a period of several centuries. Besides, the will and the opinions of human beings fluctuate; what seems right today to one man is disapproved tomorrow by another, and in that way confusion and injustice are inevitable. This is all determined by laws, and laws are unchangeable.

THE ABBOT: That is better, to be sure.

OLEARIUS: The common people do not realize this. Greedy as they are for novelties, they still utterly despise anything new that gets them out of their rut, no matter how much they may be bettered by it. They consider a lawyer as bad as a disturber of the peace, or a pickpocket, and they are furious when one thinks of establishing himself there.

LIEBETRAUT: You're from Frankfurt! I am well acquainted there. At Emperor Maximilian's coronation we stole a march or two on your lover-swains. Your name is Olearius? I don't know anyone by that name.

OLEARIUS: My father's name was Ölmann. Merely to avoid mis-

understanding on the title page of my Latin works I call myself
Olearius, according to the example and advice of worthy pro-
fessors of law.[1]

LIEBETRAUT: You did well to translate your name. A prophet is
without honor in his fatherland, and you might have had the
same experience in your mother tongue.[2]

OLEARIUS: That was not the reason.

LIEBETRAUT: Everything has more than one cause.

THE ABBOT: A prophet is without honor in his fatherland!

LIEBETRAUT: And do you know why, reverend Sïr?

THE ABBOT: Because he was born and brought up there.

LIEBETRAUT: True! That may be one reason. The other is because
on closer acquaintance with the gentlemen the halo of vener-
ability and holiness disappears which misty distance shed about
them, and then they are nothing but little stubs of tallow.

OLEARIUS: It seems as though you are appointed to pronounce
truths.

LIEBETRAUT: Since I have the heart for it, I don't lack for mouth.

OLEARIUS: But you do lack the knack of bringing them out appropriately.

LIEBETRAUT: Cupping-glasses are appropriately applied when
they draw blood.

OLEARIUS: You can tell a barber-surgeon by his apron and you
are not offended by anything in their trade. As a precaution,
you would do well to wear a cap-and-bells.

LIEBETRAUT: Where did you graduate from? It's only by way of in-
quiry so that, if the notion ever took me, I could go straight to
the right manufacturer.

---

[1] Ölmann and Olearius are German and Latin respectively for "oil man."
Prominent sixteenth century Germans often translated their names into Latin
or Greek. Goethe's maternal ancestors had thus Latinized their names of
Weber ("weaver") as Textor.

[2] *Matthew* 13:57: "A prophet is not without honour, save in his own
country . . ."

OLEARIUS: You are impudent.

LIEBETRAUT: And you are putting on a lot of airs.

(The Bishop and the Abbot laugh.)

THE BISHOP: Change of subject!—Not so hot, gentlemen. At table, anything goes.—Another topic, Liebetraut!

LIEBETRAUT: Opposite Frankfurt there's a thing called Sachsenhausen. . . .[1]

OLEARIUS *(to the Bishop)*: What are people saying about the Turkish campaign, Your Princely Grace?

THE BISHOP: The Emperor has no more urgent concern than, first, to pacify the realm, abolish feuds, and confirm the authority of the courts. Then, they say, he will proceed in person against the enemies of the empire and of Christendom. Right now his private affairs are still giving him plenty to do, and the empire, in spite of some forty proclamations of peace, is still a den of slaughter. Franconia, Swabia, the upper Rhine, and the adjacent territories are being laid waste by bold and insolent knights. Sickingen, Selbitz with his one leg, and Berlichingen with his iron hand make mockery of Imperial authority in those regions.

THE ABBOT: Yes, and if His Majesty doesn't do something about it soon, those fellows will wind up with someone in the bag.

LIEBETRAUT: That would have to be *some* fellow, to try to shove the Fulda wine-cask in the bag.[2]

THE BISHOP: That last one in particular has been my implacable enemy for many a year and annoys me beyond words. But that won't go on much longer, I hope. The emperor is now holding court in Augsburg. We have taken steps, and we cannot fail.— Doctor, do you know Adelbert von Weislingen?

OLEARIUS: No, Your Eminence.

---

[1]Sachsenhausen was proverbial for the rudeness of its inhabitants.

[2]"The Fulda wine-cask" is the obese Abbot himself. Liebetraut's remark must be an aside to the audience.

THE BISHOP: If you will wait for this man's arrival you will be delighted to see in one person the noblest, most intelligent, and most agreeable of knights.

OLEARIUS: He must be an excellent man to deserve such encomiums from such lips.

LIEBETRAUT: He was never at any academy.

THE BISHOP: We know that.

(The servants run to the window.)

What is the matter?

A SERVANT: Färber, Weislingen's squire, is just riding through the castle gate.

THE BISHOP: See what he brings. He must be announcing him.

(Exit Liebetraut.
They rise and drink another cup.)
(Reenter Liebetraut.)

THE BISHOP: What news?

LIEBETRAUT: I wish somebody else had to tell you. Weislingen has been captured.

THE BISHOP: O!

LIEBETRAUT: Berlichingen abducted him near Haslach, and three squires besides. One escaped to report it to you.

THE ABBOT: A regular Job's messenger.

OLEARIUS: I am heartily sorry.

THE BISHOP: I want to see the squire. Bring him up.—I want to talk to him myself. Bring him to my study.

(Exit.)

THE ABBOT *(sitting down)*: Another swallow.
(The servants pour wine for him.)

OLEARIUS: Would Your Reverence not desire to take a little stroll into the garden?

Post coenam stabis
Seu passus mille meabis.[1]

LIEBETRAUT: Quite true. Sitting isn't healthy for you. You will
have another stroke.

(The Abbot rises.)

(to himself) If I can just get him outdoors I'll guarantee his
exercise.

(Exeunt.)

*

[SCENE 5]

Jaxthausen.

Maria. Weislingen.

MARIA: You say you love me. I readily believe it, and I hope to
be happy with you and to make you happy.
WEISLINGEN: I feel nothing except that I am yours entirely.

(He puts his arms around her.)

MARIA: I beg you, let me go. I allowed you a kiss as a pledge. But
you seem to be trying to take possession already of what is
yours only on certain conditions.
WEISLINGEN: You are too strict, Maria! Innocent love pleases the
Deity instead of offending Him.
MARIA: Be it so. But I am not edified by such. I was taught that
caresses were like chains, strong by dint of their interconnec-
tion, and that girls, when they are in love, are weaker than
Samson after the loss of his hair.
WEISLINGEN: Who taught you that?

---

[1]After supper rise
Or take a thousand paces exercise.

MARIA: The Abbess of my convent. I was with her until into my sixteenth year, and only with you do I feel the happiness that I enjoyed in her company. She had loved and could talk. She had a heart full of sensitivity. She was a wonderful woman.

WEISLINGEN: Then she was like you! (*He takes her hand.*) What will become of me if I have to leave you!

MARIA (*drawing back her hand*): You will be a little depressed, I hope, because I know how I will be. But you must go.

WEISLINGEN: Yes, Dearest, and I will. Because I realize what bliss I shall gain by that sacrifice. Blessed be your brother and the day when he set out to capture me!

MARIA: My heart was full of hope for him and for you. "Farewell," he said upon departure, "I will see that I find him again."

WEISLINGEN: He did. How I wish I had not neglected the management of my estates and their safety by my accursed life at court! You could be mine right away.

MARIA: Postponement too has its joys.

WEISLINGEN: Don't say that, Maria, or I shall have to be afraid that your feelings are less strong than mine. But I deserve the penance. And what hopes will accompany me at every step! To be all yours, to live only in you and in the sphere of the Good; far away, cut off from the world, to taste all delights that two such hearts can furnish to each other! What is the favor of princes, what is the world's approval, compared to this one simple happiness? I have hoped and wished for a great deal, but this befalls me beyond all my hopes and wishes.

(Enter Götz.)

GÖTZ: Your page is back. He could hardly speak a word for exhaustion and hunger. My wife is giving him something to eat. I understood this much: the Bishop won't release the lad; Imperial commissioners are to be named and a day set when the affair can be settled. Be that as it may however, you are free, Adelbert. I ask nothing further but your hand that in the future you will neither publicly nor secretly give aid to my enemies.

WEISLINGEN: Here I take your hand. From this moment on let friendship and trust be between us unalterably, like an eternal law of Nature! At the same time allow me to take this hand (*He takes Maria's hand.*) and possession of this noblest of girls.

GÖTZ: May I say Yes for you?

MARIA: If you will say it with me.

GÖTZ: We are fortunate in having advantages that go together this time. You need not blush. Your looks are sufficient proof. All right then, Weislingen! Take each other's hands, and I will say Amen.—My friend and brother!—I thank you, sister. You can do more than spin hemp. You have wound a thread to hold this bird-of-Paradise. You don't look quite free, Adelbert. What's the matter? I—am completely happy. What I had hoped for only in dreams I now behold, and I am as if in a dream. Ah! now my dream comes out. Last night I thought I gave you my right iron hand, and you held me so tight that it came out of the brassarts as if it had been broken off. I was terrified and woke up at that point. I would only have needed to go on dreaming and I would have seen how you grafted a new living hand upon me.—Now you must leave me to put your castles and estates in perfect condition. The accursed court has made you neglect both. I must call for my wife. Elizabeth!

MARIA: My brother is at the peak of joy.

WEISLINGEN: And yet I can challenge him for that rank.

GÖTZ: You will live delightfully.

MARIA: Franconia is a blessed land.

WEISLINGEN: And I can say that my castle lies in the most blessed and delightful of districts.

GÖTZ: That you can, and I will confirm it. Here flows the Main,

and gently rises the hill clad in fields and vineyards and
crowned with your castle. Then the river suddenly bends and
disappears around the turn behind the cliffs of your castle. The
windows of the great hall look steep down to the water with a
view many hours into the distance.

(Enter Elizabeth.)

ELIZABETH: What is going on?

GÖTZ: You must lend your hand to this too, and say: "God bless
you!" They are a couple.

ELIZABETH: So fast!

GÖTZ: But not unexpectedly.

ELIZABETH: May you always yearn for her as you have till now,
while you were wooing her! And then! May you be as happy as
you hold her dear!

WEISLINGEN: Amen! I desire no happiness except under that head.

GÖTZ: The bridegroom, my dear wife, is making a little journey,
for the big change entails many small ones in turn. He is with-
drawing first of all from the episcopal court in order to allow
the friendship to cool little by little. Then he will wrest his
lands out of the hands of selfish tenants. And. . . . Come, sister;
come, Elizabeth. We shall leave him alone. Doubtless his page
has private business with him.

WEISLINGEN: Nothing that you cannot hear.

GÖTZ: No need.—Franconia and Swabia, you are now closer of
kin than ever. What a hold we shall keep on those princes!

(The three go out.)

WEISLINGEN: God in Heaven! Can it be that You have granted
me such bliss in my unworthiness? It is too much for my heart.
The way I hung upon those wretched people whom I fancied
I controlled, and on the glances of the prince, and on reveren-
tial approval around me! Götz, dear old Götz, you have given
me back to myself; and Maria, you make the transformation of

my mind complete. I feel as free as if I were in the bright air. Bamberg I will not see again, I will cut all the shameful ties that held me beneath myself. My heart expands. Here is no toilsome straining after greatness denied. As sure as anything, only he is happy and great who has neither to command nor to obey in order to be something!

(Enter Franz.)

FRANZ: Greetings to my gracious lord! I bring you so many greetings that I don't know where to begin. Bamberg and everyone for ten miles around send you a thousand greetings.

WEISLINGEN: Welcome, Franz! What else do you bring?

FRANZ: You stand in such remembrance at court and everywhere else as it is impossible to express.

WEISLINGEN: That won't last long.

FRANZ: As long as you live. And after your death it will shine brighter than the brass letters on a tombstone. How they took your misfortune to heart!

WEISLINGEN: What did the Bishop say?

FRANZ: He was so eager to know that he held up my answer with the zealous speed of his questions. As a matter of fact, he already knew about it, because Färber, who had escaped from Haslach, brought him the news. But he wanted to know everything. He asked with such concern whether you were not injured. I said, "He is quite unharmed, from the tips of his hair to his little toe nail."

WEISLINGEN: What did he say to the proposals?

FRANZ: He wanted to turn over everything at once—the page, and money besides, just to get you free. But when he heard that you were going to get off without that and that your word alone was going to do as much as releasing the page, he absolutely insisted on having Berlichingen brought to trial. He told me a hundred things to say to you—but I have forgotten them again. There was a long sermon on the text: "I can't get along without Weislingen."

WEISLINGEN: He'll have to learn how!

FRANZ: How do you mean? He said, "Make him hurry! Everything waits for him."

WEISLINGEN: It will have to wait. I am not going to court.

FRANZ: Not going to court? Sir! How can you think of such a thing? If you knew what I know! If you could only dream of what I have seen!

WEISLINGEN: What has come over you?

FRANZ: Just the mere recollection of it sets me beside myself. Bamberg is Bamberg no longer. An angel in woman's form is making it the antechamber of Heaven.

WEISLINGEN: Nothing more than that?

FRANZ: I'll turn monk if you see her and are not beside yourself.

WEISLINGEN: Who is she?

FRANZ: Adelheid von Walldorf.

WEISLINGEN: Her! I've heard a good deal about her beauty.

FRANZ: Heard? That's as if you said, "I've seen music." It is just as impossible for the tongue to express a line of her perfection, because in her presence the eye itself is inadequate.

WEISLINGEN: You're out of your senses.

FRANZ: That may well be. The last time I saw her I had no more senses than a drunken man. Or rather I should say that at that moment I felt as saints must feel at the sight of celestial apparitions: all the senses keener, higher, more perfect, and yet the use of none of them.

WEISLINGEN: This is odd.

FRANZ: As I was taking leave of the Bishop she was sitting with him. They were playing chess. He was very gracious, held out his hand for me to kiss, and said a number of things of which I heard nothing. For I was looking at his companion. She had her eyes fixed on the board as if she were meditating a major move. A line of subtle watchfulness about her mouth and cheek! I might have been the white king. Nobility and kindliness prevailed upon her brow. And the dazzling light of her countenance and of her bosom, how it was set off by her dark hair!

WEISLINGEN: You've turned into a downright poet over it.

FRANZ: At that moment I felt what it is that makes a poet: a full heart, a heart totally filled with one emotion! As the Bishop concluded and I was bowing, she looked at me and said, "A greeting from me as well though I have not met him. Tell him to come soon. New friends are waiting for him, and he should not scorn them because he is already so rich in old ones."—I started to make some reply, but the channel from heart to tongue was choked. I made a bow. I would have given my entire fortune to be allowed to kiss the tip of her little finger. As I stood there the Bishop knocked a pawn off the table. I went after it and in picking it up I touched the hem of her garment. A shock went through all my limbs, and I don't know how I managed to get out the door.

WEISLINGEN: Is her husband at court?

FRANZ: She has already been a widow for four months. To divert her mind she is staying in Bamberg. You will see her. When she looks at anyone it's as though one were standing in spring sunlight.

WEISLINGEN: It would have a lesser effect on me.

FRANZ: I hear you are as good as married.

WEISLINGEN: I wish I were. My gentle Maria will create my life's happiness. Her sweet soul is mirrored in her blue eyes. And white as an angel of Heaven, composed of innocence and love, she guides my heart to rest and delight. Pack up! And then: to my castle! I will not see Bamberg, not if Saint Vitus in person wanted me to.

(Exit.)

FRANZ: Now God prevent that! We'll hope for the best. Maria is gracious and beautiful, and I can't take it amiss in a captive and a sick man for falling in love with her. In her eyes there is comfort, sympathetic melancholy.—But around you, Adelheid, there is life, fire, spirit.—I would . . . !—I am a fool . . . One glance from her made me so. My lord must go down there! I must go down there! And there I will gape myself sane again, or else completely insane.

ACT II

[Scene 1]

Bamberg. A hall.

The Bishop and Adelheid are playing chess. Liebetraut with a zither; ladies and courtiers gathered around him by the fireplace.
LIEBETRAUT (*plays and sings*):

>With arrow and bow,
>With torch aglow,
>Swept Cupid a-down
>To wage a brave war
>And triumph afar
>And conquer renown.
>>Up! Up!
>>On! On!
>His weapons, they stirred,
>His pinions, they whirred,
>And fierce was his frown.
>
>But there he found hearts
>So defenseless, alas—
>They took him so gladly
>Onto their laps—
>He flung down his arrows
>On the hearth in a heap;
>They kissed him and held him
>And rocked him to sleep.
>>Hei ei o! Popeio!

ADELHEID: Your mind is not on the game. Checkmate!
THE BISHOP: There's still a way out.

ADELHEID: You won't go on much longer. Checkmate!

LIEBETRAUT: If I were a great lord I wouldn't play this game, and I would prohibit it at court and throughout the country.

ADELHEID: It's true, this game is a touchstone of the intellect.

LIEBETRAUT: That's not the reason! I would rather hear the howl of a death-knell and of evil-omened birds, I would rather hear the barking of the growling watchdog Conscience, and hear them through the deepest slumber, than hear chess-bishops and chess-knights and the rest of those animals with their everlasting "Checkmate!"

THE BISHOP: Who would ever think up such a thing?

LIEBETRAUT: Someone, for example, that was weak and had a strong conscience, the way those two things usually go together. They call it a royal game and say it was invented for a king who rewarded the inventor with an ocean of abundance. If that is true, I feel as though I saw him before me. He was a minor either in brains or in years, under the tutelage of his mother or his wife, he had baby-hair in his beard and flax at his temples, he was pliant as a willow-shoot, and he liked to play checkers with the ladies[1]—not out of passion, God forbid!— but just as a pastime. His tutor, too active to be a scholar and too stiff to be a man of the world, invented the game *in usum Delphini*[2] because it was so like His Majesty—and so forth.

ADELHEID: Checkmate!—You ought to fill in the gaps in our history books, Liebetraut.

(They get up.)

LIEBETRAUT: The gaps in our genealogical trees, that would be more profitable. Since the achievements of our ancestors and their portraits serve one and the same purpose, namely to dec-

---

[1] "Checkers" and "ladies" are both *Damen* in German.
[2] *In usum Delphini*—(Latin) "for the use of the Dauphin," a phrase applied to specially expurgated texts used in the education of the heir to the throne of France.

orate the empty walls of our rooms and of our characters, there would really be some point in that.

THE BISHOP: He will not come, you say?

ADELHEID: I beg you, dismiss it from your mind.

THE BISHOP: What can it be?

LIEBETRAUT: What? The reasons can be ticked off like rosary-beads. He has fallen into a kind of contrition, of which I'd like to cure him fast.

THE BISHOP: Do that. Ride over to see him.

LIEBETRAUT: My errand?

THE BISHOP: Anything whatsoever. Stop at nothing if you can get him back.

LIEBETRAUT: May I also bring you into it, my Lady?

ADELHEID: With discretion.

LIEBETRAUT: That's a big order.

ADELHEID: Do you know me so little, or are you too young to know in what tone you have to talk to Weislingen about me?

LIEBETRAUT: In the tone of a quail-call, I imagine.

ADELHEID: You will never learn sense.

LIEBETRAUT: Does anyone, my Lady?

THE BISHOP: Go, go. Take the best horse in my stable, choose your squires, and bring him here to me.

LIEBETRAUT: If I don't charm him here, say an old woman that cures warts and freckles knows more about sympathetic powers than I do.

THE BISHOP: What good will that do? Berlichingen has taken him in completely. If he does come here, he will only want to leave again.

LIEBETRAUT: *Want*—that's no problem; but will he be *able?* The hand-clasp of a prince and the smile of a beautiful woman—no Weislingen will tear himself away from those. I go in haste and take my leave of Your Grace.

THE BISHOP: Prosperous journey!

ADELHEID: Adieu.

(He leaves.)

THE BISHOP: Once he gets here, I will be counting on you.

ADELHEID: You intend to use me as a limed twig?

THE BISHOP: Oh no!

ADELHEID: As a decoy-bird, then?

THE BISHOP: No, Liebetraut will play that part. I beg you, do
not refuse what no one else can provide!

ADELHEID: We'll see.

*

[SCENE 2]

Jaxthausen.
Hans von Selbitz. Götz.

SELBITZ: Everyone will praise you for declaring war on those
Nürnberg people.

GÖTZ: It would have eaten my heart out if I had had to go on
owing it to them for very long. It has come out that they betrayed my page to the Bambergers. They shall have reason to
think of me!

SELBITZ: They have an ancient grudge against you.

GÖTZ: And I against them. It suits me fine that they have started
something.

SELBITZ: The imperial cities and the clergy have always stuck together.

GÖTZ: They have reason to.

SELBITZ: We'll make things hot for them.

GÖTZ: I was counting on you. I wish to God the Mayor of Nürnberg with his gold chain around his neck would come our way:
he'd be surprised, for all his cleverness.

SELBITZ: I hear Weislingen is on your side again. Will he join us?

GÖTZ: Not yet. There are reasons why he can't openly give us help yet. For a while it will be enough that he is not against us. Without him, the priest is what the vestments are without the priest.

SELBITZ: When do we move out?

GÖTZ: Tomorrow or the day after. Pretty soon now there will be merchants from Bamberg and Nürnberg coming back from the Frankfurt Fair. We'll make a good catch.

SELBITZ: God willing.

(Exeunt.)

*

[SCENE 3]

Bamberg. Adelheid's room.
Adelheid. Lady-in-waiting.

ADELHEID: He is here, you say? I can hardly believe it.

LADY-IN-WAITING: If I hadn't seen him myself, I would say I doubted it.

ADELHEID: The Bishop can have Liebetraut mounted in gold. He has achieved a masterpiece.

LADY-IN-WAITING: I saw him as he was about to ride in the castle gate. He was on a white horse. The horse shied as it came to the drawbridge and would not budge. The people had come running up out of all the streets to see him. They were delighted at the horse's misbehavior. From all sides they hailed him, and he thanked them all. He sat his mount with a pleasing composure, and with coaxing and threatening he finally got it through the gate, Liebetraut with him and a few attendants.

ADELHEID: How do you like him?

LADY-IN-WAITING: As I have liked few men. He resembled the Emperor here *(pointing to Maximilian's portrait)* as if he were his son. Only his nose was somewhat smaller, just such friendly light brown eyes, just such fine blond hair, and built like a god. A half melancholy look on his face—I don't know—pleased me so much.

ADELHEID: I'm curious to see him.

LADY-IN-WAITING: There would be a gentleman for you.

ADELHEID: Silly fool!

LADY-IN-WAITING: Children and fools. . . .

(Enter Liebetraut.)

LIEBETRAUT: Well, my Lady, what do I deserve?

ADELHEID: Horns from your wife. For by her account you have lured many a neighbor's honorable housewife from her duty.

LIEBETRAUT: Not at all, my Lady! *To* her duty, you mean. For if it did happen, I lured her to her husband's bed.

ADELHEID: How did you manage to get him here?

LIEBETRAUT: You know perfectly well how fools are caught. Am I supposed to teach you *my* tricks besides?—First I pretended I knew nothing, understood nothing about his conduct, and thereby put him at the disadvantage of telling the whole story. Right away I saw it from a completely different angle from his, I could not agree—could not understand—and so on. Then I talked all sorts of stuff about Bamberg hit and miss, great things and small things, revived certain old memories, and when I had his imaginative powers engaged, I really tied up again a number of threads that I found broken. He didn't know what was coming over him, he felt a new urge toward Bamberg, he desired . . . without desiring. Then, when he got to consulting his heart and tried to sort all those things out and was much too concerned with himself to be on his guard, I threw a rope around his neck woven of three powerful strands: women's favor, princes' favor, and flattery—and with it dragged him here.

ADELHEID: What did you say about me?

LIEBETRAUT: The simple truth. That you were having unpleas-
antnesses over your estates—that you hoped that since he had
so much influence with the Emperor, he might easily put an
end to these.

ADELHEID: Very well.

LIEBETRAUT: The Bishop will bring him to you.

ADELHEID: I will be waiting for them . . .

(Exit Liebetraut.)

. . . with such a heart
as I have seldom waited for any visitor.

*

[SCENE 4]

In the Spessart Forest.
Berlichingen. Selbitz. Georg in squire's dress.

GÖTZ: You didn't find him, Georg?

GEORG: He had ridden to Bamberg the day before with Liebetraut, and two squires along.

GÖTZ: I don't see what that will come to.

SELBITZ: I do. Your reconciliation was a little too sudden to be
lasting. That Liebetraut is a sly rascal. He let himself to talked
into it by him.

GÖTZ: Do you think he'll prove faithless to his alliance?

SELBITZ: The first step has been taken.

GÖTZ: I don't believe it. Who knows how necessary it may have
been for him to go to court? People are still indebted to him.
We shall hope for the best.

SELBITZ: Let's hope to God he deserves it and does the best!

GÖTZ: A stratagem just occurs to me. Let's put Georg into that
smock we took from the Bamberg outrider and give him the

safe-conduct pass. He can ride over to Bamberg and see how things stand.

GEORG: I've hoped for this for a long time.

GÖTZ: It will be your first mission. Be careful, lad! I'd hate to have you meet with an accident.

GEORG: Don't worry! It won't put me off if ever so many are crawling around me: to me they're like rats and mice.

(Exit.)

*

[SCENE 5]

Bamberg.
The Bishop. Weislingen.

THE BISHOP: You do not wish to be kept here any longer?

WEISLINGEN: You would not like to have me break my oath.

THE BISHOP: I would have liked not to have you swear it. What kind of a spirit possessed you? Was I not able to set you free without that? Do I count for so little at the Imperial court?

WEISLINGEN: It is done now. Forgive me if you can.

THE BISHOP: I don't understand what on earth obliged you to take that step! Give me up? Weren't there a hundred other terms on which to escape? Don't we have his page? Wouldn't I have given him money enough and quieted him? Our designs against him and his associates would have been dropped . . . Oh, I forget that I am talking with his friend who is now working against me and who can easily disengage the mines that he himself has set.

WEISLINGEN: My Lord!

THE BISHOP: And yet—now that I see your face again, hear your voice. . . . It is not possible, not possible.

WEISLINGEN: Farewell, my Lord.

THE BISHOP: I give you my blessing. Formerly when you used to go away I would say: Till we meet again! Now—God grant we never see each other again!

WEISLINGEN: Many things can change.

THE BISHOP: Perhaps I shall see you once more—as an enemy before my walls laying waste the fields that now have you to thank for their flourishing condition.

WEISLINGEN: No, my Lord.

THE BISHOP: You cannot say No. The secular estates, my neighbors, all have it in for me. As long as I had you. . . . Go, Weislingen! I have nothing more to say to you. You have undone many things. Go!

WEISLINGEN: And I don't know what I can say.

(Exit the Bishop.
Enter Franz.)

FRANZ: Adelheid is waiting for you. She is not well. And yet she does not want to let you go without farewell.

WEISLINGEN: Come.

FRANZ: Are we really leaving?

WEISLINGEN: This very evening.

FRANZ: I feel as if I were departing from the world.

WEISLINGEN: So do I. And what's more, as if I didn't know where I was going to.

*

[SCENE 6]

Adelheid's room.
Adelheid. Lady-in-waiting.

LADY-IN-WAITING: You look pale, my Lady.

ADELHEID: I do not love him and yet I wish he were staying. You

see, I could live with him although I would not like to have
him for a husband right away.

LADY-IN-WAITING: Do you think he will go?

ADELHEID: He is at the Bishop's to say good-bye.

LADY-IN-WAITING: He has another hard stand to make after that.

ADELHEID: How do you mean?

LADY-IN-WAITING: Can you ask, my Lady? You have his heart on
your hook, and if he tries to tear himself loose he will bleed to
death.

(Enter Weislingen. [The lady-in-waiting retires.])

WEISLINGEN: You are not well, my Lady?

ADELHEID: You cannot care about that. You are leaving us, leaving us forever. Why should you ask whether we live or die?

WEISLINGEN: You misjudge me.

ADELHEID: I take you as you present yourself.

WEISLINGEN: Appearances deceive.

ADELHEID: Are you a chameleon?

WEISLINGEN: If you could see my heart!

ADELHEID: Pretty things would meet my eye.

WEISLINGEN: Indeed they would! You would find your picture in
it.

ADELHEID: In some nook or other along with the portraits of ex-
tinct families. I beg you, Weislingen, to realize you are talking
with me. False words are most valid when they serve as masks
for our actions. A masker who is recognizable plays a sorry role.
You do not deny your actions and yet you say the opposite.
What is anyone to make of you?

WEISLINGEN: Whatever you will. I am so plagued with what I *am*
that I am not much concerned about what people may take
me for.

ADELHEID: You have come to say good-bye.

WEISLINGEN: Allow me to kiss your hand and I will say farewell.

You remind me. I didn't realize . . . I am being tiresome, my Lady.

ADELHEID: You misconstrue me. I wanted to help you on your way—for you do want to be on your way.

WEISLINGEN: O, say I must. If I were not compelled by my knightly obligation, by my solemn hand-clasp. . . .

ADELHEID: Go! Go! Tell that to girls that read *Teuerdank* and want a man like that.[1] Knightly obligation! Children's nonsense!

WEISLINGEN: You don't mean that.

ADELHEID: Upon my oath, you're pretending! What have you promised? And to whom? To a man who fails to recognize his obligation to the Emperor and to the empire you incur obligation at precisely the moment when he incurs the ban of outlawry by the act of taking you prisoner. Incur obligation that can be no more valid than the oath illegally obtained under duress! Don't our laws release us from such vows? Talk stuff like that to children that believe in Rübezahl.[2] There are other things behind this. To turn enemy of the state, enemy of civil peace and welfare! Enemy of the Emperor! A brigand's partner! You, Weislingen, with your gentle soul!

WEISLINGEN: If you only knew him . . .

ADELHEID: . . . I would do him justice. He has a lofty, intractable soul. For that very reason woe to you, Weislingen! Go and imagine you are his partner! Go and let yourself be dominated! You are affable, obliging. . . .

WEISLINGEN: So is he.

ADELHEID: But you are yielding and he is not. He will sweep you away unawares, you will be the slave of a nobleman when

---

[1]*Teuerdank* is an allegorical romance of chivalry outlined by Emperor Maximilian and composed by his secretary, depicting Maximilian's own suit for the hand of Maria of Burgundy; published 1517.

[2]Rübezahl—a waggish mountain sprite of the Riesengebirge, somewhat resembling Robin Goodfellow.

you could be master over princes.—But it is cruelty to spoil
your taste for your future status.

WEISLINGEN: If you had only felt how graciously he treated me!

ADELHEID: Graciously! You credit him with that? It was his duty.
And what would you have lost if he had been disagreeable? To
me that would have been more welcome. A haughty man like
him. . . .

WEISLINGEN: You're speaking about your enemy.

ADELHEID: I was speaking for your liberty—and I really don't
know what advantage there is in that for me. Good-bye!

WEISLINGEN: Allow me one more moment.

(He takes her hand and remains silent.)

ADELHEID: Have you anything further to say to me?

WEISLINGEN: — — I must be going.

ADELHEID: Then go!

WEISLINGEN: My Lady! . . . I cannot.

ADELHEID: You must.

WEISLINGEN: Is this to be the last sight of you?

ADELHEID: Go. I am ill, most inopportunely.

WEISLINGEN: Don't look at me like that.

ADELHEID: You decide to be our enemy and we are supposed to
smile? Go!

WEISLINGEN: Adelheid!

ADELHEID: I hate you!

(Enter Franz.)

FRANZ: My Lord, the Bishop is calling for you.

ADELHEID: Go on! Go on!

FRANZ: He begs you to come quickly.

ADELHEID: Go on! Go on!

WEISLINGEN: I will not say good-bye. I shall see you again!

(Exit.)

ADELHEID: See me again? We shall prevent that. Margarete, if he comes, turn him away. I am ill, I have a headache, I am asleep . . . Turn him away! If he is still to be won, that will be the way to do it!

(Exit.)

＊

[SCENE 7]

An antechamber.
Weislingen. Franz.

WEISLINGEN: She will not see me?
FRANZ: It is getting dark. Shall I saddle the horses?
WEISLINGEN: She will not see me?
FRANZ: For when does Your Grace order the horses?
WEISLINGEN: It is too late. We shall stay here.
FRANZ: Thanks be to God!

(Exit.)

WEISLINGEN: You're staying? Be on your guard. The temptation is great. My horse shied as I was about to come in the castle gate. My good angel blocked his way, knowing the perils that awaited me here.—And yet it is not right not to put the many affairs that I left unfinished for the Bishop into some order at least, so my successor will be able to take up where I left off. And I can do that much without harm to Berlichingen and our alliance. For keep me here they shall not.—Would have been better, though, if I hadn't come. But I will get off—to-morrow, or the day after.

(Exit.)

＊

[Scene 8]

In the Spessart Forest.
Götz. Selbitz. Georg.

Selbitz: You see, it went just as I said.

Götz: No! No! No!

Georg: Please believe the news I bring you is true. I did as you
ordered, took the Bamberger's smock and his safe-conduct pass,
and to earn my food and drink besides, I escorted Reineck
peasants up to Bamberg.

Selbitz: In that disguise? That could have gone badly with you.

Georg: I realize that now too, afterwards. A horseman that thinks
ahead of time won't take any very broad jumps. I got to Bamberg, and the first thing I heard at the inn was that Weislingen
and the Bishop had made up and that there was much talk of
a marriage with von Walldorf's widow.

Götz: Gossip.

Georg: I saw him escorting her to table. She is beautiful, by my
oath, she is beautiful! We all bowed. She thanked us all. He
nodded his head and looked very pleased. They passed on, and
the crowd murmured, "A handsome couple!"

Götz: That may be.

Georg: Listen further. The next day as he was on his way to
Mass, I watched my chance. He was alone with a page. I was
standing at the foot of the steps and I said to him softly, "A
word or two from your Berlichingen!" He was startled; I saw
the confession of his crime on his face. He scarcely had the
heart to look at me—me, a mere squire.

Selbitz: That was because his conscience was lower than your
rank.

Georg: "You're a Bamberger?" said he.—"I bring you greetings
from Knight Berlichingen," said I, "and I am supposed to

ask . . ."—"Come to my room tomorrow morning," said he, "and we'll talk further."

Götz: Did you go?

Georg: Of course I went, and it was a long, long while that I had to stand out in the antechamber. And the lads in silk eyed me front and back. I thought: "Go ahead and stare!" Finally I was ushered in. He seemed angry, but I didn't care. I stepped up to him and carried out my errand. He acted furiously angry, like someone that didn't have the stomach for it and didn't want it to show. He was amazed that you should take him to task through the intermediary of a squire. That made me mad. I said there were only two kinds of people, honest men and rascals, and I served Götz von Berlichingen. Then he started in and talked all kinds of silly stuff, which amounted to this: You had rushed him, he was under no obligation to you, and he didn't want to have anything to do with you.

Götz: You have that from his own lips?

Georg: That and more besides.—He threatened me . . .

Götz: That's enough! So he is lost now too! Faith and Trust, you have deceived me again. Poor Maria! How will I break the news to you!

Selbitz: I'd rather lose my other leg too than be a son of a bitch like that.

(Exeunt.)

*

[Scene 9]

Bamberg.
Adelheid. Weislingen.

Adelheid: The time begins to hang unbearably heavy. I don't

feel like talking and I am ashamed to play with you. Boredom, you are worse than a cold fever.

WEISLINGEN: Are you tired of me already?

ADELHEID: Not so much of you as your company. I wish you were where you wanted to go and we had not kept you back.

WEISLINGEN: Such is woman's favor! First she hatches out our fondest hopes with maternal warmth, then like a fickle hen she leaves the nest and abandons her already growing progeny to death and corruption.

ADELHEID: Blame it on women! The reckless gambler chews and stamps on the cards that made him lose in all innocence. But let me tell you something about men. Who are you to talk about fickleness? You, who are rarely what you claim to be and never what you ought to be. Kings in holiday robes, envied by the mob. What would a tailor's wife give to wear around her neck a string of pearls from the hem of your garment that is contemptuously kicked aside by your heels!

WEISLINGEN: You're bitter.

ADELHEID: It is the antistrophe of your ode. Before I knew you, Weislingen, I was like the tailor's wife. Rumor, hundred-tongued, and not metaphorically speaking, had so quack-doctor-touted you that I let myself be talked into wishing: "Wouldn't you just love to get a look at that quintessence of the male sex, that Phoenix Weislingen!" My wish was granted.

WEISLINGEN: And the Phoenix turned out to be an ordinary barn-yard rooster.

ADELHEID: No, Weislingen, I was interested in you.

WEISLINGEN: It seemed so . . .

ADELHEID: And was. For you really did surpass your reputation. The mob prizes only the reflection of merit. Just as I have a way of not liking to think about people to whom I wish well, just that way we lived for a time side by side. Something was lacking, and I didn't know what it was I missed in you. Finally

my eyes were opened. Instead of the active man who enlivened
the affairs of a princedom, who did not lose sight of himself
and his fame in so doing, who had climbed to the clouds over
a hundred great enterprises as over mountains piled one on
top of the other, I saw all of a sudden someone complaining
like a sick poet, as melancholy as a healthy girl, and idler than
an old bachelor. At first I attributed it to your misfortune,
which lay fresh upon your heart, and excused you as well as
I could. Now that it seems to be getting worse with you from
day to day, you will have to forgive me if I tear my favor away
from you. You possess it without right, I gave it to someone
else for life who was unable to transfer it to you.

WEISLINGEN: Then set me free.

ADELHEID: Not before all hope is lost. In these circumstances
solitude is dangerous.—Poor man, you are as dejected as one
whose first girl has proven unfaithful, and just for that reason
I will not give you up. Give me your hand, forgive me for what
I have said out of love.

WEISLINGEN: If you could only love me, if you could only grant
one drop of comfort to my ardent passion! Adelheid! Your ac-
cusations are terribly unjust. If you had any notion of the
hundredth part of what has been seething within me all this
time, you would not have mangled me so mercilessly this way
and that way with favor and indifference and contempt . . .
You smile! . . . Coming to terms with myself again after that
overhasty step cost me more than *one* day. To struggle against
the man whose memory is so vividly fresh in my love!

ADELHEID: Strange man, who can love someone whom you envy!
It's as if I brought provisions to my enemy.

WEISLINGEN: I realize that delay will not do in this case. He is
informed that I am once again Weislingen, and he will avail
himself of his advantage over us. Besides, Adelheid, we are not
so sluggish as you think. Our horsemen are reenforced and

alert, our negotiations are proceeding, and we hope the Imperial Diet in Augsburg will bring our projects to fruition.

ADELHEID: You're going there?

WEISLINGEN: If I could take some hope with me!

(He kisses her hand.)

ADELHEID: O ye of little faith! Always signs and wonders![1] Go, Weislingen, and complete the work. The Bishop's advantage, yours, mine, they are so intertwined that, even if it were only for the sake of policy . . .

WEISLINGEN: You can jest.

ADELHEID: I am not jesting. The haughty Duke is holding my estates; Götz will not leave yours unharassed for very long; and if we do not stick together like our foes and do not get the Emperor over on our side, we are lost.

WEISLINGEN: I am not worried. The biggest share of the princes are of our opinion. The Emperor wants help against the Turks and for that reason it is proper for him to support us again. What a joy it will be for me to liberate your estates from haughty enemies, to lay the restless heads in Swabia back on their pillows, to restore the peace of the bishopric and of us all! And then . . . ?

ADELHEID: One day leads to another, and the future is in the hands of Fate.

WEISLINGEN: But we have to want it.

ADELHEID: Well, we do want it.

WEISLINGEN: You're sure?

ADELHEID: Why, yes. Go.

WEISLINGEN: Enchantress!

---

[1] *John* 4:48—"Except ye see signs and wonders, ye will not believe."

❋

[Scene 10]

An inn. A peasant wedding. Music and dancing outside.
The bride's father, Götz, and Selbitz at table. The bridegroom
steps up to them.

GÖTZ: The most sensible thing was that you brought your quarrel
to such a happy and fortunate end by means of a marriage.

THE BRIDE'S FATHER: Better than I had dared dream. Peace and
quiet with my neighbor, and a daughter well provided for
besides.

THE BRIDEGROOM: And I in possession of the disputed land, and
the prettiest Miss in the whole town as well. I wish to God you
had intervened sooner.

SELBITZ: How long have you been at this lawsuit?

THE BRIDE'S FATHER: Going on eight years. I'd rather have the
ague twice that time as start in again from the beginning. It's
a tussle, you wouldn't believe it, to drag a verdict out of those
curliwigs' hearts.[1] And what have you got when you're through?
Devil take that Assessor Sapupi![2] He's a damned black Italian.

THE BRIDEGROOM: Yes, he's a mad one. I was there twice.

THE BRIDE'S FATHER: And I three times. And see, Gentlemen,
we finally do get a verdict, one where I am as much in the right
as he is, and he as much as I am, and we stood there with our
mouths hanging open until the Lord God prompted me to
give him my daughter and the land too in the bargain.

GÖTZ *(drinking a toast)*: Good trials in the future.

THE BRIDE'S FATHER: God grant! Come what may, however, I'll
never go to law again as long as I live. What a pile of money
it takes! You have to pay for every bow the attorney makes you.

---

[1]The artificial curled wigs of lawyers were worn in Goethe's eighteenth,
but not in Götz's sixteenth, century.

[2]"Sapupi" is an anagram of Papius, a bribe-taking assessor discharged from
the Imperial Court in Wetzlar just before young lawyer Goethe arrived to
work there in 1772.

SELBITZ: Well, there *are* Imperial inspection tours annually.

THE BRIDE's FATHER: Never heard of them. But many a sweet Thaler went for extras. Such bleeding you never heard of!

GÖTZ: How do you mean?

THE BRIDE's FATHER: Oh, there they all hold out a hollow paw. The assessor alone, God forgive him! got eighteen Gulden in gold out of me.

THE BRIDEGROOM: Who?

THE BRIDE's FATHER: Sapupi! Who else?

GÖTZ: It's a shame.

THE BRIDE's FATHER: All right, I had to pay down twenty to him. And when I had counted them out for him in his garden house—which is magnificent—in the big main hall, my heart fairly broke for grief. For look, a man's house and home stand firm, but where is ready cash to come from? I stood there, God knows what came over me. I didn't have a red cent in my purse for travel money. Finally I worked up the courage and put it up to him. Then he saw my soul was turning to water and he threw two of them back down for me and sent me off.

THE BRIDEGROOM: That's not possible! Sapupi?

THE BRIDE's FATHER: Why look that way! Of course! Nobody else!

THE BRIDEGROOM: Devil take him! He got fifteen Gulden in gold out of me too.

THE BRIDE's FATHER: Damnation!

SELBITZ: Götz, *we* are robbers!

THE BRIDE's FATHER: That's why the verdict came out so lopsided. You dog!

GÖTZ: You mustn't let this go unreported.

THE BRIDE's FATHER: What are we supposed to do?

GÖTZ: Start out for Speyer. It's inspection time right now. Make a complaint. They have to investigate it and help you get what is yours.

THE BRIDEGROOM: Do you think we'll get it through?

GÖTZ: If I could get him by the ears, I'd promise you you would.

SELBITZ: The amount is well worth a try.

GÖTZ: I've ridden out before this for one fourth the amount.

THE BRIDE'S FATHER: What do you think?

THE BRIDEGROOM: We will, come what may.

(Enter Georg.)

GEORG: The Nürnbergers are on their way.

GÖTZ: Where?

GEORG: If we ride nice and gently, we'll grab them in the woods between Beerheim and Mühlbach.

SELBITZ: Fine!

GÖTZ: Come on, children! God be with you! Help us all to get what is ours!

THE PEASANT: Many thanks. You won't stay on for supper?

GÖTZ: We can't. Good-bye.

ACT III

[SCENE 1]

Augsburg. A garden.
Two Nürnberg merchants.

FIRST MERCHANT: Here we will stand, for here the Emperor has to pass by. He is just coming up the long path.
SECOND MERCHANT: Who is with him?
FIRST MERCHANT: Adelbert von Weislingen.
SECOND MERCHANT: Bamberg's friend! That's good.
FIRST MERCHANT: We'll fall on our knees, and I will do the talking.
SECOND MERCHANT: Good. There they come.

(Enter the Emperor and Weislingen.)

FIRST MERCHANT: He looks annoyed.
THE EMPEROR: I am depressed, Weislingen, and when I look back on my past life I could well turn despondent—so many enterprises half accomplished, so many that came to naught, and all because there is not a prince in the empire who is not so small but that he is more concerned about his own whims than about my ideas.

(The merchants cast themselves at his feet.)

THE MERCHANT: Serenest Highness! High and Mighty!
THE EMPEROR: Who are you? What is it?
THE MERCHANT: Poor merchants from Nürnberg, Your Majesty's servants, who implore your aid. Götz von Berlichingen and Hans von Selbitz have set upon thirty of our number in the Bamberg safe-conduct area as they were on their way back from

62

the Frankfurt Fair and robbed them. We beg Your Imperial Majesty for help, for support; otherwise we shall all be ruined men compelled to beg our bread.

THE EMPEROR: God in Heaven! God in Heaven! What is this? One of them has only one hand, the other only one leg. If they ever had two hands and two legs what would you do then?

THE MERCHANT: We most submissively request Your Majesty to cast a compassionate eye upon our hard pressed circumstances.

THE EMPEROR: The way things go! If a merchant loses a bag of pepper the whole empire is supposed to be called out, and if there is business to be done of great moment to Imperial Majesty and to the empire, involving kingdoms, princedoms, dukedoms, then there is not a soul to be rounded up.

WEISLINGEN: You come at an inopportune time. Go now and wait here for a few days.

BOTH MERCHANTS: We commend us to Your Grace.

(Exeunt.)

THE EMPEROR: More troubles again! They keep growing like the Hydra's heads.

WEISLINGEN: And they won't be exterminated except by fire and sword and by an energetic campaign.

THE EMPEROR: You think so?

WEISLINGEN: I consider nothing more practicable, if Your Majesty and the princes could agree on other insignificant differences. It is by no means all of Germany that is complaining about disturbance. Franconia and Swabia alone still show fire in the ashes from what is left of the destructive internecine civil war. And even there there are many nobles and freemen who yearn for peace. If we could just get this Sickingen, this Selbitz—this Berlichingen out of the way, the rest would soon collapse of themselves. For *they* are the ones whose spirit stirs up the rebellious crowd.

THE EMPEROR: I should like to spare those men; they are brave and noble. If I were fighting a war they would have to take the field with me.

WEISLINGEN: One could wish they had long since learned to respond to their obligations. Then, too, it would be extremely dangerous to reward their rebellious enterprises with positions of honor. For it is precisely this Imperial gentleness and clemency that they have so monstrously misused up to now; and their followers, who are setting their hope and trust on it, cannot be brought under control until we have annihilated them completely in the eyes of the world and cut off totally any hope they may have of ever getting back up again.

THE EMPEROR: You recommend severity, then?

WEISLINGEN: I see no other means of eliminating the giddy folly that grips whole provinces. Do we not already hear in this place and in that place the bitterest complaints of the nobles to the effect that their subjects, their serfs are revolting against them and disputing with them and threatening to diminish their traditional sovereignty, so that the most dangerous consequences are to be feared?

THE EMPEROR: This would be a fine opportunity to move against Berlichingen and Selbitz; only, I wouldn't want them to come to any harm. I would like to have them taken captive, and then they would have to swear their oath of truce to stay quietly in their castles and not to leave their jurisdictions. At the next session I will propose it.

WEISLINGEN: A joyous acclamation of approval will spare Your Majesty the end of the speech.

(Exeunt.)

*

[SCENE 2]

Jaxthausen.
Sickingen. Berlichingen.

SICKINGEN: Yes, I have come to ask your noble sister for her heart and hand.

GÖTZ: Then I wish you had come sooner. I must tell you: during his captivity Weislingen won her love, sued for her hand, and I promised her to him. I let him loose, that caged bird, and he scorns the kindly hand that fed him in time of distress. He is flitting about, God knows on what hedge, looking for his food.

SICKINGEN: Is this true?

GÖTZ: As I say.

SICKINGEN: He broke a double bond. It's well for you that you did not become related any closer with the traitor.

GÖTZ: She sits there, the poor girl, grieving and praying her life away.

SICKINGEN: We'll make her sing.

GÖTZ: What? Can you make up your mind to marry a girl that has been deserted?

SICKINGEN: It is an honor for both of you to be betrayed by him. Is the poor girl supposed to enter a convent because the first man she knew was a good-for-nothing? Not at all! I insist on her becoming the queen of my castles.

GÖTZ: I tell you she was not indifferent to him.

SICKINGEN: Don't you think I'm capable of driving away the shadow of a scoundrel? Let's go and see her.[1]

(Exeunt.)

*

---

[1]The historical Franz von Sickingen, 1481-1523, a champion of the Reformation and a friend of Martin Luther, was far more distinguished politically and militarily than Götz von Berlichingen, into whose family he did not marry.

[SCENE 3]

Camp of the Imperial Ban Enforcement.
A Captain. Officers.

THE CAPTAIN: We must go cautiously and spare our troops as much as possible. Besides, we have express orders to corner him and take him alive. That will take some doing, for who is going to tackle him?

FIRST OFFICER: Right! And he will fight back like a wild boar. Never in his life has he done us any harm, and every man will avoid risking arms and legs to please the Emperor and the empire.

SECOND OFFICER: It would be a shame if we didn't capture him. If I once get him by the collar he won't get away.

FIRST OFFICER: Just don't grab him with your teeth: he might rip your jaw off. My dear young Sir, people of that sort are not to be grabbed like runaway thieves.

SECOND OFFICER: We'll see.

THE CAPTAIN: He must have our letter by now. We mustn't put off sending out a patrol to observe him.

SECOND OFFICER: Let me lead it.

THE CAPTAIN: You're not familiar with the area.

SECOND OFFICER: I have a groom that was born and brought up here.

THE CAPTAIN: I'm satisfied with that.

(Exeunt.)

*

[SCENE 4]

Jaxthausen.
Sickingen.

SICKINGEN: Everything is going just as I hoped. She was a bit

startled at my proposal and looked me over from head to foot.
I'll bet she was comparing me with that whitefish of hers.[1]
Thank God I can stand the comparison! Her answer was brief
and confused. All the better! Let her simmer a while yet. With
girls that are parboiled in unhappy love, a proposal of marriage cooks done fast.

(Enter Götz.)

What news, my friend?

Götz: Proclaimed an outlaw!

Sickingen: What?

Götz: Here, read this edifying letter. The Emperor has ordered
activation of the ban against me, which is supposed to carve my
flesh for the birds beneath the heaven and the beasts upon the
field.

Sickingen: They'll go to them first. I'm here at just the right
time.

Götz: No, Sickingen, you must leave. Your great projects might
be ruined if you started to turn enemy of the state at so inopportune a time. Besides, you will be of much more use to
me if you appear to be neutral. The Emperor likes you, and
the worst that can happen to me will be to be taken prisoner.
Then come forward with your intercession and pull me out
of the mess into which untimely help could plunge us both.
What good would it do? The expedition is on its way to
attack me. If they find you are with me, they will only send
more men, and we will be no better off. The Emperor is at
the source, and I would be irrevocably lost if bravery could be
breathed into men as fast as a posse can be blown together.

Sickingen: At least I can secretly send over twenty horsemen or
so to join you.

Götz: Good. I have already sent Georg for Selbitz and my fol-

---

[1]A *Weisling* is a kind of small white fish.

lowers in the vicinity. When I get my men together, old boy, they will be a company the like of which few princes have ever seen gathered.

SICKINGEN: You will be few against their numbers.

GÖTZ: One wolf is too many for a whole flock of sheep.

SICKINGEN: But what if they have a good shepherd?

GÖTZ: Don't worry! They're nothing but hirelings. And then, the best knight can't do anything when he is not master of his actions. They came against me once before this way, when I had promised to serve the Count Palatine against Konrad Schotte. He handed me a memorandum from the Chancery about how I was supposed to ride and behave. I threw the paper back at the Councillors and said I wouldn't know how to follow its directions; I didn't know what I might run into, *that* wasn't in the memorandum; I had to keep my own eye peeled and see for myself what I had to do.

SICKINGEN: Good luck, Brother! I'll be off right away, and I'll send you whatever I can scare up in a hurry.

GÖTZ: See the ladies yet before you go. I left them together. I wanted you to have her word before you left. Then send me the horsemen and come back secretly to pick up Maria. For my castle, I fear, will soon be no place for women.

SICKINGEN: We'll hope for the best.

(Exeunt.)
*

[SCENE 5]

Bamberg. Adelheid's room.
Adelheid. Franz.

ADELHEID: Then both enforcement expeditions have already started out?

FRANZ: Yes, and my lord has the pleasure of attacking your enemies. I wanted right away to go along, however glad I was to come to see you. And now I want to start right off again in order to come back soon with happier news. My lord has given me permission.

ADELHEID: How are things with him?

FRANZ: He is cheerful. He bade me kiss your hand.

ADELHEID: There . . . Your lips are warm.

FRANZ *(to himself, pointing to his bosom)*: It's still warmer here. *(Aloud)* My Lady, your servants are the most fortunate people under the sun.

ADELHEID: Who is the leader against Berlichingen?

FRANZ: The lord of Sirau. Farewell, best and gracious Lady. I must be off again. Do not forget me.

ADELHEID: You must eat and drink something, and rest.

FRANZ: What need? I have seen you. I am neither weary nor hungry.

ADELHEID: I know your faithfulness.

FRANZ: Oh, my Lady!

ADELHEID: You can't stand it. Take some rest and eat a little something.

FRANZ: Your concern for a poor youth!

(Exit.)

ADELHEID: There are tears in his eyes. I love him with all my heart. No one has ever been so genuinely and so warmly attached to me.

(Exit.)

*

[SCENE 6]

Jaxthausen.
Götz. Georg.

GEORG: He wants to talk to you himself. I don't know him. He is an imposing man with fiery black eyes.

GÖTZ: Bring him in.

(Enter Lerse.)

GÖTZ: God's greeting to you! What do you bring?

LERSE: Myself. That isn't much, but all there is I offer you.

GÖTZ: You are welcome, doubly welcome. A brave man, and just at this time when I didn't dare hope to gain new friends but rather feared the loss of old ones from hour to hour. Give me your name.

LERSE: Franz Lerse.

GÖTZ: I thank you, Franz, for making me acquainted with a brave man.

LERSE: I introduced myself to you once before, but that time you didn't thank me for it.

GÖTZ: I don't recall you.

LERSE: I'm sorry. Do you still remember how you became enemies with Konrad Schotte on account of the Count Palatine and started out to ride to Hassfurt for the Mardi Gras?

GÖTZ: I remember it well.

LERSE: Do you recall how on the way you encountered twenty-five horsemen near a village?

GÖTZ: Right. I thought at first there were only twelve of them and divided my band—there were sixteen of us—and stopped near the village behind the shed intending to let them go by. Then I was going to go after them, as I had arranged with the other group.

LERSE: But we saw you and rode up a hill near the village. You rode past and stopped down below. When we saw you weren't going to come up, we rode down.

GÖTZ: Only then did I notice that I had stuck my hand into the coals. Twenty-five against eight! There was no dilly-dallying then. Erhard Truchsess ran a squire of mine through, and for that I charged him right off his horse. If they had all held out

like him and one squire, it would have gone hard with me
and my little band.

LERSE: The squire of whom you said . . .

GÖTZ: He was bravest I had seen. He went after me hot and
heavy. Every time I thought I had beaten him off and was
about to take on some others, there he was at me again and
thrusting away furiously. He jabbed me through the vambrace
too so that he grazed my arm a little.

LERSE: Have you forgiven him?

GÖTZ: I liked him only too well.

LERSE: Well, I just hope you will be satisfied with me. I did my
demonstration performance on you yourself.

GÖTZ: Are you the one? O welcome!—Maximilian, can you say
that among the men serving you you enlisted a single one this
way!

LERSE: I'm surprised you didn't figure me out sooner.

GÖTZ: How was I supposed to imagine that anyone would offer
me his services who had tried like the worst of enemies to
conquer me?

LERSE: Just that very fact, Sir! From my youth up I have served
as a squire and I have pitted my strength against many a knight.
When we ran up against you I was glad. I knew your name
and then I came to know you. You know I didn't hold out, but
you saw it wasn't from fear, because I kept coming right back
again. In short, I got to know you, and from that time on I
made up my mind to serve you.

GÖTZ: How long do you want to serve with me?

LERSE: For a year. Without pay.

GÖTZ: No, you shall be maintained like anyone else, and what's
more, like the man that gave me such a rough time of it at
Remlin.

(Enter Georg.)

GEORG: Hans von Selbitz sends you his greetings. He will be here tomorrow with fifty men.

GÖTZ: Good.

GEORG: A detachment of Imperials is coming down along the Kocher,[1] doubtless to reconnoitre your position.

GÖTZ: How many?

GEORG: Fifty of them.

GÖTZ: Is that all? Come on, Lerse, we'll knock hell out of them so, when Selbitz comes, he'll find one job done.

LERSE: That'll be a plentiful early vintage.

GÖTZ: To horse!

(Exeunt.)

*

[SCENE 7]

A forest at the edge of a swamp.
Enter two Imperials, meeting.

FIRST SQUIRE: What are you doing here?

SECOND SQUIRE: I got permission to answer the call of Nature. Since the false alarms of last night it's hit me in the bowels so I have to dismount every two minutes.

FIRST SQUIRE: Is the detachment stationed near by?

SECOND SQUIRE: A good hour up the woods.

FIRST SQUIRE: Then how do you come to be wandering down here?

SECOND SQUIRE: I beg you not to betray me. I want to get to the nearest village and see if I can't cure my trouble with warm compresses. Where do you come from?

FIRST SQUIRE: From the next village. I've picked up some wine and bread for our officer.

---

[1]The Kocher is a small river parallel to the Jaxt.

SECOND SQUIRE: So! He gets himself something good right before our faces and we're supposed to go hungry! A fine example!

FIRST SQUIRE: Come on back with me, you sneak!

SECOND SQUIRE: The fool I'd be! There are a lot more in the detachment that would be glad to go hungry if they were as far away from it as I am.

FIRST SQUIRE: Do you hear? Horses!

SECOND SQUIRE: O my God!

FIRST SQUIRE: I'll climb this tree.

SECOND SQUIRE: I'll hide among the reeds.

(Enter Götz, Lerse, Georg, and squires on horseback.)

GÖTZ: On past the pond here and left into the woods. That way we'll come around behind them.

(They ride on.)

FIRST SQUIRE *(climbs down from the tree.)*: It's no good there. Michel! He doesn't answer? Michel, they're gone! *(He walks over to the swamp.)* Michel! My God! He's sunk out of sight. Michel! He doesn't hear me, he's smothered. So you died anyway, you coward!—We're beaten. Enemies, enemies everywhere!

(Enter Götz and Georg on horseback.)

GÖTZ: Halt there, you, or you're a dead man!

THE SQUIRE: Spare my life!

GÖTZ: Your sword! Georg, lead him to the other captives that Lerse has down on the edge of the woods, I've got to overtake their fugitive leader.

(Exit.)

THE SQUIRE: What has become of our knight that was leading us?

GEORG: My master knocked him head over heels off his horse so his plume stuck in the mire. His horsemen lifted him onto his horse and off they went like mad!

(Exeunt.)

*

[Scene 8]

Camp.
The Captain. The first knight.

FIRST KNIGHT: They're fleeing toward camp from way out.

THE CAPTAIN: He must be at their heels. Have fifty men sent out as far as the mill. If he extends himself too far maybe you will catch him.

(Exit the knight.
Enter the second knight, led in.)

How are things with you, young Sir? Did you lose a couple of points off your antlers?

THE KNIGHT: Plague take you! The strongest antlers would have splintered like glass. You devil! He charged me and I felt as if a thunderbolt were driving me into the ground.

THE CAPTAIN: Thank God you got away at all.

THE KNIGHT: No thanks are called for. A couple of my ribs are in two. Where is the surgeon?

(Exeunt.)

*

[Scene 9]

Jaxthausen.
Götz. Selbitz.

GÖTZ: What do you say to the outlawry proclamation, Selbitz?

SELBITZ: It's Weislingen's doings.

GÖTZ: You think?

SELBITZ: I don't think, I know.

GÖTZ: From where?

SELBITZ: He was at the Imperial Diet, I tell you; he was around the Emperor.

Götz: All right, then we'll undo another of his plots.
Selbitz: Let's hope so.
Götz: We're off, and let the rabbit hunt begin.

*

[Scene 10]
Camp.
The Captain. Knights.

The Captain: We're getting nowhere this way, gentlemen. He will knock out one detachment after another for us, and everyone that doesn't get killed or captured will rather go running in God's name over to Turkey than back to camp. That way we'll get weaker every day. We must close in on him once and for all, and in earnest. I will be there myself and he shall see who it is he has to deal with.

A knight: That's satisfactory to all of us. Only, he is so familiar with the district, knows every path and trail in the mountains, that he's no more to be caught than a mouse in a granary.

The Captain: We'll get him just the same. First, on to Jaxthausen. Willy-nilly, he'll have to come up to defend his castle.

A knight: Is our whole detachment to march?

The Captain: Of course! Don't you know we're melted down by a hundred as it is?

A knight: Let's move fast then, before the whole ice-block thaws out. It's warm around here and we're like butter in the sun.

(Exeunt.)
*

[Scene 11]
Mountain and forest.
Götz. Selbitz. A detachment of soldiers.

Götz: They're coming in full force. It's high time Sickingen's horsemen made a junction with us.

SELBITZ: Let's divide up. I will go left around the hill.

GÖTZ: Good. And you, Franz, take the fifty up through the woods to the right. They'll come across the heath, and I will hold against them. Georg, you will stay with me. And when you see them attack me, don't lose any time hitting their flanks. We'll splash them. They don't think we can give them any opposition.

(Exeunt.)

*

[SCENE 12]

The heath, with a hill on one side and a forest on the other.
The Captain. The Ban enforcement column.

THE CAPTAIN: He's stopping on the heath! That's impertinent. He'll pay for it. What! Not be afraid of the river rushing down on him?

THE KNIGHT: I wouldn't like to have you ride at the head of the column. He looks as if he'd plant the first man to hit him upside down in the ground. Ride behind.

THE CAPTAIN: I don't like to.

THE KNIGHT: I beg you. You are still the knot that holds this scourge of hazel rods together; untie it, and he will lop you off one by one like sedge grass.

THE CAPTAIN: Blow, trumpeter, and blow him away!

(Exeunt.)
(Enter Selbitz at a gallop from behind the hill.)

SELBITZ: Follow me! They're going to shout to their hands: "Be multiplied!"

(Exit.)
(Enter Lerse out of the forest.)

LERSE: To Götz's aid! He's almost surrounded. Brave Selbitz, you have already broken through. We'll strew the heath with their thistle-tops.

(He rides on.
Tumult.)

*

[SCENE 13]

A hill with a watchtower.
Selbitz wounded. Squires.

SELBITZ: Lay me down here and go back to Götz.

FIRST SQUIRE: Let us stay, Sir! You need us.

SELBITZ: One of you climb the watchtower and see how things are going.

FIRST SQUIRE: How am I going to get up?

SECOND SQUIRE: Stand on my shoulders. Then you can reach the hole and boost yourself up through the opening.

FIRST SQUIRE *(climbs up.)*: Oh, Sir!

SELBITZ: What do you see?

FIRST SQUIRE: Your horsemen are fleeing toward the hill.

SELBITZ: The damned scoundrels! I wish they were standing firm and I had a bullet through my head. One of you ride over and curse and damn them back!

(Exit a squire.)

Do you see Götz?

THE SQUIRE: I see his three black plumes in the midst of the turmoil.

SELBITZ: Swim, brave swimmer! *I* lie here!

THE SQUIRE: A white plume. Who is that?

SELBITZ: The Captain.

THE SQUIRE: Götz forces his way to him . . . wham! Down he goes.

SELBITZ: The Captain?

THE SQUIRE: Yes, Sir.

SELBITZ: Fine! Fine!

THE SQUIRE: Oh! I don't see Götz any longer.

SELBITZ: Then die, Selbitz!

THE SQUIRE: A terrific crush where he was standing. Georg's blue plume has disappeared too.

SELBITZ: Come down. You don't see Lerse?

THE SQUIRE: Nothing. Everything is all mixed up.

SELBITZ: No more! Come! How are Sickingen's horsemen holding up?

THE SQUIRE: Good.—There goes somebody fleeing toward the woods. Another one! A whole detachment! Götz is gone.

SELBITZ: Come down.

THE SQUIRE: I can't.—Good! Good! I see Götz! I see Georg!

SELBITZ: On horseback?

THE SQUIRE: High on their horses! We've won! We've won! They're running away!

SELBITZ: The Imperials?

THE SQUIRE: Their banner in the midst of them, and Götz after them. They're scattering. Götz overtakes the standard bearer . . . He has the banner . . . He's stopping. A handful of men around him. My friend has caught up with him . . . They're riding this way.

(Enter Götz, Georg, Lerse, and a detachment of soldiers.)

SELBITZ: Welcome, Götz! Victory! Victory!

GÖTZ *(dismounting)*: A costly one! A costly one! You're wounded, Selbitz?

SELBITZ: You are alive and victorious! I did very little. And those dogs of horsemen of mine! How did you get away?

GÖTZ: It was a hot one this time! And I have Georg here to thank for my life, and Lerse here to thank for it. I knocked the Captain off his nag. They struck my horse down and rushed at me. Georg cut his way through to me and jumped off; I like a lightning flash was up on his nag, and he like a thunderclap was mounted again too. How did you come by that horse?

GEORG: I ran my dagger into the guts of some fellow that was slashing at you, just as his armor was raised up. He went down, and helped you free of a foe and myself to a horse.

GÖTZ: There we were, stuck, till Franz beat his way in to us, and then we mowed ourselves out from the inside.

LERSE: Those dogs I was leading were supposed to mow their way in from the outside until our scythe-blades met, but they fled like Imperials.

GÖTZ: Friend and foe both fled. Only you, my little band, kept the rear open. I had enough to do with the boys in front of me. Their Captain's fall helped me shake them, and they ran for it. I have their banner and a few prisoners.

SELBITZ: The Captain got away from you?

GÖTZ: They had rescued him in the meantime. Come on, children! Come on, Selbitz!—Make a stretcher out of boughs.— You can't get on a horse. Come to my castle. They're scattered. But we are few, and I don't know whether they have any troops to send back. I'll put you up, my friends. A glass of wine will taste good after a scrap like this.

*

[Scene 14]

Camp.

THE CAPTAIN: I could kill you all with my own hands! What! Run away! He didn't have a handful of men left! Run away from one man! Nobody will believe it, except those that enjoy laughing at us.—Ride around, you, and you, and you. Wherever you find any of our scattered troops, bring them back or strike them down. We've got to hone these stains off even if our swords are ruined in the process.

*

[SCENE 15]

Jaxthausen.
Götz. Lerse. Georg.

GÖTZ: We mustn't delay a single minute! Poor lads, I dare not offer you any rest. Hunt around quickly and try to scare up more horsemen. Have them all gather at Weilern. They will be safest there. If we delay, they'll move up before my castle.
(Exeunt Lerse and Georg.)
I've got to send out one on reconnoissance. Things are beginning to get hot. If they were brave fellows . . . ! But, as things stand, it's their numbers.
(Exit.)
(Enter Sickingen and Maria.)

MARIA: I beg you, dear Sickingen, do not leave my brother! His horsemen and Selbitz' and yours are all scattered; he is alone, Selbitz has been taken wounded to his castle, and I fear the worst.

SICKINGEN: Be calm. I won't leave him.
(Enter Götz.)

GÖTZ: Come to the church, the priest is waiting. In a quarter of an hour you shall be a married couple.

SICKINGEN: Let me stay here.

GÖTZ: Right now to the church with you.

SICKINGEN: Gladly.—And afterwards?

GÖTZ: Afterwards you shall go your way.

SICKINGEN: Götz!

Götz: You don't want to go to the church?
Sickingen: Come on! Come on!

*

[Scene 16]

Camp.
The Captain. The knight.

The Captain: How many are they all told?
The knight: A hundred and fifty.
The Captain: Out of four hundred! That's bad. Up now and straight to Jaxthausen before he gets his breath again and meets us on the road.

*

[Scene 17]

Jaxthausen.
Götz. Elizabeth. Maria. Sickingen.

Götz: God bless you and give you happy days, and may He keep for your children those that He takes away from you.
Elizabeth: And may He make them as you are: upright. Then let them be whatever they may.
Sickingen: I thank you. And I thank you, Maria. I have led you to the altar, and you shall lead me to happiness.
Maria: We shall make a pilgrimage together to that strange promised land.
Götz: Prosperous journey!
Maria: We didn't mean it that way, we are not going to leave you.
Götz: You must, sister.
Maria: You are very unkind, brother!
Götz: And you more tender than provident.

(Enter Georg.)

GEORG *(privately)*: I can't scare up anyone. Just one was so inclined; afterwards he changed his mind and wouldn't.

GÖTZ: Good, Georg. My luck is beginning to turn like the weather. I suspected as much, though. *(Aloud)* Sickingen, I beg you to leave yet this evening. Persuade Maria. She is your wife. Make her realize that. When women cut across our enterprises our foes are safer in the open field than they would otherwise be in their castles.

(Enter a squire.)

THE SQUIRE *(softly)*: Sir, the Imperial column is on the march straight for here and very fast.

GÖTZ: I have stirred them up with whips. How many are they?

THE SQUIRE: About two hundred. They can't be more than two hours from here.

GÖTZ: Still across the river?

THE SQUIRE: Yes, Sir.

GÖTZ: If I just had fifty men they wouldn't get across. You didn't see Lerse?

THE SQUIRE: No, Sir.

GÖTZ: Have everybody stand by in readiness.—We must part, my dear ones. Weep, my good Maria. Moments will come when you will be glad. It is better to weep on your wedding day than that too great joy should be the herald of future misery. Farewell, Maria. Farewell, brother!

MARIA: I cannot leave you, sister. Dear brother, let us stay! Do you think so little of my husband that you scorn his help in this extremity?

GÖTZ: Yes, things have gone a long way with me. Perhaps I am near my fall. You are beginning to live, and you must cut yourselves off from my fate. I have ordered your horses saddled. You must leave at once.

MARIA: Brother! Brother!

ELIZABETH *(to Sickingen)*: Do as he says. Go!

SICKINGEN: Dear Maria, let us go.

MARIA: You too? My heart will break.

GÖTZ: Then stay. In a few hours my castle will be surrounded.

MARIA: Alas! Alas!

GÖTZ: We shall defend ourselves as best we can.

MARIA: Mother of God, have mercy on us!

GÖTZ: And in the end we will either die or surrender.—You will have wept your noble husband into one fate along with me.

MARIA: You are torturing me.

GÖTZ: Stay! Stay! We will be taken prisoner together. Sickingen, you will fall into the pit with me. I was hoping you would help me out of it.

MARIA: We will go. Sister! Sister!

GÖTZ: Get her to safety, and then remember me.

SICKINGEN: I will not share her bed until I know that you are out of danger.

GÖTZ: Sister . . . dear sister! *(Kisses her.)*

SICKINGEN: Away! Away!

GÖTZ: Just one minute more . . . I will see you again. Be comforted. We shall meet again.

(Exeunt Sickingen and Maria.)

I drove her away, and now that she is going I would like to keep her here. Elizabeth, you will stay with me!

ELIZABETH: Till death!

(Exit.)

GÖTZ: Whom God loves, to him may He give a wife like that!

(Enter Georg.)

GEORG: They're near by, I saw them from the tower. The sun was rising and I saw their pikes gleaming. As I saw them I was no more frightened than a cat before an army of mice. We are playing the part of the rats.

GÖTZ: Look after the bolts on the gate. Barricade it on the inside with beams and rocks.

(Exit Georg.)

We'll fool their patience, and their bravery they shall chew away on their own fingernails.

(A trumpeter from outside.)

Aha! Some red-coat scoundrel who is going to put the question before us whether we intend to show the white feather.

(He goes to the window.)

What's this?

(A voice is heard speaking in the distance.)

(in his beard) A noose around your neck!

(The trumpeter goes on speaking.)

Offender of Majesty!—A priest put in that provocation.

(The trumpeter concludes.)

(answering) Surrender? Unconditionally? Whom are you talking to! Am I a brigand? Tell your Captain this: Before Imperial Majesty I have, as always, all due respect. But as for him, tell him he can kiss my arse!

(He slams the window shut.)

*

[SCENE 18]

Siege. The kitchen.
Elizabeth. Götz, entering.

GÖTZ: You have a lot of work, my poor wife.

ELIZABETH: I wish I had it for a long time to come. We can hardly hold out very long.

Götz: We didn't have time to lay in provisions.

Elizabeth: And all those people that you were always feeding. We're already running low on wine too.

Götz: If we can only hold out to a certain point, so they propose capitulation! We'll do them some fine damage. They'll shoot all day long and wound our walls and smash our window-panes. Lerse is a brave lad. He'll slip around with his gun, and wherever one of them ventures too near . . . Bang! He's a goner.

(Enter a squire.)

The squire: Coals, my Lady.

Götz: What's the matter?

The squire: That was the last of the bullets. We're going to cast some new ones.

Götz: How are we on powder?

The squire: So-so. We're spacing our shots nicely.

*

[Scene 19]

The great hall.
Lerse with a bullet mold and the squire with coals.

Lerse: Set it there and see if you can find some lead in the house. Meanwhile I'll help myself here.

(He lifts out a window and smashes the panes.)

Every advantage counts.—That's the way in this world, nobody knows what use things can be turned to. The glazier that set these panes certainly never thought the lead might give one of his descendants a nasty headache. And when my father begot me he never thought what bird under the sky or what worm in the ground might eat me.

Georg *(enters with an eaves-trough pipe.)* : There's lead for you. If you hit them with just half of it, there won't one of them get away to report to His Majesty: Lord, we made a poor showing.

LERSE *(cutting off a chunk)*: A nice piece.

GEORG: Let the rainwater look for a new path. I'm not afraid of it. A brave horseman and proper rain will get through anywhere.

LERSE *(pours.)*: Hold the ladle. *(He goes to the window.)* There's one of those Imperial boys going around with a gun. They think we're out of ammunition. He can sample this bullet hot off the griddle.

(He loads.)

GEORG *(lays the ladle up against the mold.)*: Let me see.

LERSE *(fires.)*: I got my sparrow.

GEORG: He was firing at me before ... *(They pour.)* ... as I was climbing out the attic window to get the eaves-trough. He hit a pigeon sitting not far from me; it dropped into the eaves-trough. I thanked him for the roast of fowl and climbed back in with double booty.

LERSE: We'll load up now and go around through the whole castle earning our dinner.

(Enter Götz.)

GÖTZ: Wait, Lerse, I've got something to tell you. I won't keep you, Georg, from your hunting.

(Exit Georg.)

They're offering me a truce.

LERSE: I'll go out to them and hear what it amounts to.

GÖTZ: It will be that I am supposed to enter knightly imprisonment on certain terms.

LERSE: That won't do. How would it be if they granted us free retreat, as long as you are not expecting relief from Sickingen? We would bury all the money and silver where they would never find it with a divining rod, then turn the castle over to them and get away in good style.

Götz: They won't let us.

Lerse: Let's give it a try. We'll call for a safe-conduct and I'll go
out and see.

(Exeunt.)

*

[Scene 20]

The great hall.
Götz, Elizabeth, Georg, squires at table.

Götz: This is the way danger brings us together. Enjoy it, my
friends! Don't forget the drinking. The bottle is empty. Another one, dear wife.

(Elizabeth shrugs her shoulders.)

No more left?

Elizabeth *(softly)*: *One* more. I put it aside for you.

Götz: Oh no, my dear. Bring it out. They need fortifying. I
don't. It's my affair, you know.

Elizabeth: Bring it in from the cupboard out there.

Götz: It's the last one. And I feel as though we had no cause to
be sparing. It's a long time since I have been so satisfied.

(He pours.)

Long live the Emperor!

All: Long may he live!

Götz: That shall be our second-last word when we are dying! I
love him, for we have one and the same fate. And I am more
fortunate than he. He has to catch mice for the estates of the
empire while the rats are gnawing away at his possessions. I
know he often wishes himself dead rather than be any longer
the soul of such a crippled body.

(He pours.)

There's just enough to go around once more. And when our

blood starts on its decline the way the wine in this bottle runs first feebly and then drop by drop . . . *(He lets the last drops fall into his glass.)* . . . what shall our last word be?

GEORG: Long live Freedom!

GÖTZ: Long live Freedom!

ALL: Long live Freedom!

GÖTZ: And if *she* survives us we can die in peace. For in our minds we see our grandchildren happy and our grandchildren's Emperor happy. If the servers of the princes served as nobly and freely as you serve me, if the princes served the Emperor as I would like to serve him . . .

GEORG: Then things couldn't help but be very different.

GÖTZ: Not so much as it might seem. Haven't I known excellent men among the princes, and can it be the stock has died out? Good men, who were happy in themselves and in their subjects, who could stand to have a free and noble neighbor beside them and neither fear him nor envy him, whose hearts rejoiced when they saw many of their equals around their tables, and who didn't first have to transform knights into court-toadies before they could live with them.

GEORG: Have you known such lords?

GÖTZ: Indeed I have! As long as I live I'll never forget how the Landgrave of Hanau gave a hunting party, and the princes and lords who were there ate under the open sky, and the countryfolk all hurried over to see them. It was no masquerade he had arranged in his own honor. But the full, round heads of the lads and lasses, all those red cheeks, and the prosperous men and stately oldsters, happy faces every one of them, and how they shared in the splendor of their master, who was enjoying himself on God's ground in their midst.

GEORG: That was a lord as perfect as you.

GÖTZ: Oughtn't we to hope that more such princes can some day rule, that reverence for the Emperor, peace and friendship

of neighbors, and love of subjects will be the most precious
heritage that can pass on to grandsons and great-grandsons?
Every man would keep what belonged to him and increase it
within itself, instead of the way they now think they are not
prospering if they are not destroying others.

GEORG: Would we have any missions to ride after that?

GÖTZ: Please God there wouldn't be any uneasy heads in all of
Germany! We would still find enough to do. We would clear
the wolves out of the mountains, we would fetch a roast out of
the forest for our peacefully tilling neighbor and in return
would eat soup with him. If that would not be enough, we
would emplace ourselves together with our brothers like cheru-
bim with flaming swords at the boundaries of the empire, against
those wolves the Turks, against those foxes the French, and at
the same time protect our dear Emperor's very exposed provinces and the tranquillity of the empire. What a life that
would be, Georg, when a man could risk his skin for the gen-
eral welfare!

(Georg leaps up.)

Where are you going?

GEORG: Oh, I forgot we were hemmed in . . . and the Emperor
has hemmed us in . . . and to get away with our whole skins,
we will risk our skins.

GÖTZ: Be of good courage.

(Enter Lerse.)

LERSE: Freedom! Freedom! Those are bad men, indecisive, cau-
tious asses. You are to withdraw with weapons, horses, and
armor. The provisions you will have to leave behind.

GÖTZ: They won't bring on a toothache chewing on them.

LERSE *(privately)*: Have you hidden the silver?

GÖTZ: No! Wife, go with Franz. He has something to say to you.

(Exeunt.)

*

[SCENE 21]

The castle courtyard.
Georg in the stable, singing.

GEORG: There was a bird caught by a boy
                            Hm! Hm!
                    Who on the cage did gloat for joy.
                            Hm! Hm!
                            So! So!
                            Hm! Hm!
                    So silly was his glee,
                            Hm! Hm!
                    He grabbed so clumsily,
                            Hm! Hm!
                            So! So!
                            Hm! Hm!
                    Out flew the tom-tit to a house
                            Hm! Hm!
                    And laughed his fill at foolish louts.
                            Hm! Hm!
                            So! So!
                            Hm! Hm!

GÖTZ: How are things going?

GEORG *(leads his horse out.)*: They're saddled.

GÖTZ: You're fast.

GEORG: As the bird out of the cage.

                    (Enter all the besieged persons.)

GÖTZ: You have your guns? Oh, no! Go up and get the best ones
    out of the gun-racks. It won't cost any more. We'll ride ahead.

GEORG: Hm! Hm!
                            So! So!
                            Hm! Hm!
                    (Exeunt.)
                            *

[SCENE 22]

The great hall.
Two squires at the gun-rack.

FIRST SQUIRE: I'll take this one.

SECOND SQUIRE: I this one. There's a better one still.

FIRST SQUIRE: No, no! Hurry up and come on!

SECOND SQUIRE: Listen!

FIRST SQUIRE *(runs to the window.)*: Help, merciful God! They're murdering our master. He's down off his horse! Down goes Georg!

SECOND SQUIRE: Where shall we flee? Along the wall, down the walnut tree, and into the field.

(Exit.)

FIRST SQUIRE: Franz is still holding them off. I'll go help him. If they die, I don't care to live.

(Exit.)

ACT IV

[SCENE 1]

An inn at Heilbronn.
Götz.

GÖTZ: I feel like the evil spirit that the Capuchin conjured into a sack.[1] I wear myself out and accomplish nothing. The perjurors!

(Enter Elizabeth.)

What news, Elizabeth, of my beloved loyal men?

ELIZABETH: Nothing definite. Some were cut down, some are in prison. No one could or would name them more specifically for me.

GÖTZ: Is this the reward of loyalty, of childlike obedience?—Well may you fare and long may you live on earth!

ELIZABETH: Dear husband, do not chide our heavenly Father. They have their reward, it was born into them, a free and noble heart. Let them be captive: they are free! Heed the deputation of Councilors. Their great golden chains suit their countenances. . . .

GÖTZ: Like pearls on swine.—I'd like to see Georg and Franz shut up!

ELIZABETH: It would be a sight to make the angels weep.

GÖTZ: I wouldn't weep. I would clench my teeth and chew the cud of my fury. In chains, those apples of my eye! You dear lads, if you hadn't loved me!—I could not get my fill of gazing at them.—Not to keep their word given in the Emperor's name!

---

[1]Troublesome ghosts were trapped by monks in bags or boxes and deported by hand to remote places.

ELIZABETH: Dismiss these thoughts. Consider that you are about to appear before the Councilors. You are in no state of mind to meet them properly, and I fear the worst.

GÖTZ: What do they mean to charge me with?

ELIZABETH: The Court Summoner!

GÖTZ: Justice' jackass! Lugs their sacks to mill and their dung out to the field. What is it?

(Enter the Court Summoner.)

THE COURT SUMMONER: The Lords Commissioner are assembled at the City Hall and have sent for you.

GÖTZ: I'm coming.

THE COURT SUMMONER: I will accompany you.

GÖTZ: A big honor.

ELIZABETH: Restrain yourself.

GÖTZ: Have no fear.

(Exeunt.)

*

[SCENE 2]

The City Hall.
Imperial Councilors. The Captain. Aldermen of Heilbronn.

AN ALDERMAN: At your command we have assembled the strongest and bravest citizens. They are waiting close at hand for your signal to seize Berlichingen.

THE FIRST COUNCILOR: We shall not fail to praise, and with great pleasure, to His Imperial Majesty your readiness to comply with his supreme command.—They are artisans?

THE ALDERMAN: Smiths, wine draymen, carpenters, men with practised fists and well protected *(pointing to his chest)* here.

THE COUNCILOR: Good.

(Enter the Court Summoner.)

THE COURT SUMMONER: Götz von Berlichingen is waiting outside the door.

THE COUNCILOR: Show him in.

(Enter Götz.)

GÖTZ: God's greeting to you, gentlemen! What do you want with me?

THE COUNCILOR: First, that you reflect where you are and before whom!

GÖTZ: By my oath, I do not fail to recognize you, Sirs.

THE COUNCILOR: You do your duty.

GÖTZ: With all my heart.

THE COUNCILOR: Be seated.

GÖTZ: Down there? I can stand. That stool reeks of poor sinners,[1] just like the whole room.

THE COUNCILOR: Stand, then.

GÖTZ: To the point, if you will be so kind.

THE COUNCILOR: We shall proceed in proper order.

GÖTZ: That suits me. I wish it had always been the case.

THE COUNCILOR: You know how you passed into our hands unconditionally.

GÖTZ: What will you give me if I forget it?

THE COUNCILOR: If I could give you discretion I would help your cause.

GÖTZ: Help! If you only could! But that takes more doing than to harm it.

THE COURT CLERK: Shall I enter all this in the record?

THE COUNCILOR: Whatever has to do with the proceedings.

GÖTZ: As far as I'm concerned, you can have it printed.

THE COUNCILOR: You were in the power of the Emperor, whose paternal clemency took the place of Majesty's justice and by

---

[1]The poor sinners' stool or bench was a seat of public humiliation, usually at church, for persons convicted of certain wrongdoings.

way of abode for you designated, instead of a prison, Heilbronn, one of his beloved cities. You promised upon your oath
to appear, as beseems a knight, and to await further action
with humility.

Götz: Quite so, and I am here and I am waiting.

The councilor: And we are here to announce to you His Imperial Majesty's clemency and graciousness. He pardons your
transgressions, pronounces you free of the ban and of all well
deserved punishment, which pronouncements you will acknowledge with submissive gratitude, and in return you will repeat
the oath which shall herewith be read to you.

Götz: I am His Imperial Majesty's loyal servant as always. One
word yet before you proceed. My men, where are they? What
is to be done with them?

The councilor: That does not concern you.

Götz: Then may the Emperor turn his face away from you when
you are in distress! They were my comrades and still are.
Where have you taken them?

The councilor: We are not obliged to give you any account of
that.

Götz: Ah! I forgot that you are not even bound to what you
promise, not to mention. . . .

The councilor: Our commission is to present you with the oath.
Submit to the Emperor and you will find a way to plead for
your comrades' life and liberty.

Götz: Your memorandum!

The councilor: Clerk, read it out.

The court clerk: "I, Götz von Berlichingen, by means of this
document, publicly acknowledge that I have recently rebelled
in mutinous wise against Emperor and empire. . . ."

Götz: That is not true! I am no rebel, I have committed no
crime against His Imperial Majesty, and the empire is no concern of mine.

THE COUNCILOR: Restrain yourself and listen further.

GÖTZ: I will listen to nothing further. Let any man step forth
and testify! Have I taken a single step against the Emperor,
against the house of Austria? Have I not demonstrated at all
times by all my acts that I realized better than anyone what
obligations Germany owes its ruler, especially what lesser persons, the knights and the freemen, owe their Emperor? I would
be a scoundrel if I allowed myself to be persuaded to sign that.

THE COUNCILOR: And yet we have express orders to persuade you
amicably, or, in event of failure, to put you in prison.

GÖTZ: In prison? Me?

THE COUNCILOR: And there you can wait your fate from the
hands of the law if you will not accept it from the hands of
clemency.

GÖTZ: In prison! You are misusing Imperial power. In prison!
That is not his command. What! First—the traitors—to set a
trap for me and to bait it with their oath, their knightly word,
then to promise me knightly imprisonment and break their
promise again!

THE COUNCILOR: We are under no obligation of good faith with
a brigand.

GÖTZ: If you were not wearing the Emperor's likeness which I
venerate in its meanest counterfeit, you would eat that word
"brigand" and choke on it! I am engaged in an honorable
feud. You could thank God and parade yourself large before
the world if you had ever in your life done a deed as noble as
that for which I now sit here captive.

> (*The councilor gestures to the alderman;*
> *the latter rings a bell.*)

Not for sorry gain, and not to grab territory and subjects away
from defenseless little people, did I ride out to war, but to
liberate my page and to protect my own skin! Do you see anything wrong in that? Neither Emperor nor empire would have

noticed our distress amid their pillows. I still have, thank God, *one* hand left and I did well to use it.

*(Enter citizens with sticks in their hands
and weapons at their sides.)*

What is the meaning of this?

THE COUNCILOR: You will not listen.—Seize him!

GÖTZ: Is that your intention? Whoever isn't a Hungarian ox better not come too close to me! He'll get such a box on the ears from this right iron hand of mine as will cure him once and for all of headache, toothache, and all the other aches of this world.

*(They move toward him. He knocks one of them down and grabs
the weapon from the side of a second. They fall back.)*

Come on! It would be a pleasure to get to know the bravest among you.

THE COUNCILOR: Surrender!

GÖTZ *(sword in hand)*: Do you realize that all I have to do now is to knock my way through this bunch of rabbit-chasers and gain the open field? But I am going to teach you how a man keeps his word. Promise me knightly imprisonment and I'll turn over my sword and be your prisoner as before.

THE COUNCILOR: You propose to bargain, sword in hand, with the Emperor?

GÖTZ: God forbid! Only with you and your noble company.— You can go home, good people. For the time you have lost you will get nothing, and there is nothing to be gotten here except lumps on your heads.

THE COUNCILOR: Seize him! Doesn't your love for your Emperor give you any more courage than this?

GÖTZ: Not any more than the Emperor gives them plasters to heal the wounds that their courage might bring them.

(Enter the Court summoner.)

THE COURT SUMMONER: The tower watchman has just shouted a

column of more than two hundred men is moving on the city. They appeared unexpectedly from behind the vineyard and are threatening our walls.

THE COUNCILOR: Alas for us! What is this?

(Enter the watchman.)

THE WATCHMAN: Franz von Sickingen is at the gate and sends you word that he has heard how improperly the solemn promise to his brother-in-law was broken and how the men of Heilbronn have lent their full support. He demands an accounting, or else he will set fire to the city at all four corners within the hour and open it up to pillage.

GÖTZ: Good for my brother-in-law!

THE COUNCILOR: Withdraw, Götz.—What is to be done?

THE ALDERMAN: Have mercy on us and on our citizenry. Sickingen is ruthless in his anger, and he is the man to go through with it.

THE COUNCILOR: Are we to surrender our own and the Emperor's privileges?

THE CAPTAIN: If we only had the men to assert them. But this way we could be killed and the cause would only be that much worse off. We will gain by giving way.

THE ALDERMAN: We'll get Götz to put in a word for us. I feel as though I already saw the city in flames.

THE COUNCILOR: Show Götz in.

GÖTZ: What now?

THE COUNCILOR: You would do well to talk your brother-in-law out of his mutinous undertaking. Instead of rescuing you from destruction he will only plunge you deeper into it by putting himself in your position.

GÖTZ *(sees Elizabeth by the door and says privately to her)*: Go down and tell him to force his way in instantly and come here, only to do no harm to the city. If these rascals oppose him here,

he is to use force. I don't care if I get killed just so long as they
all get cut down with me.

*

[Scene 3]

A large room in the city hall.
Sickingen. Götz. The entire city hall is occupied by Sickingen's
troops.

Götz: That was help from Heaven. How did you happen to
come so unexpectedly and just when wanted, brother-in-law?

Sickingen: No magic to it. I had sent out two or three scouts to
hear how things were going with you. At the news of their
perjury I started out. And now we have them.

Götz: I'm not asking for anything but knightly imprisonment.

Sickingen: You are too honorable. Not even to avail yourself of
the advantage that the upright man has over perjurors! They
are in the wrong, and we're not going to put any pillows under
them. They have shamefully misused the Emperor's commands.
And if I know His Majesty, you can certainly insist on more.
This is too little.

Götz: I have always been satisfied with little.

Sickingen: And have always gotten the short end. My opinion is
that they should let your squires out of prison and let you and
them together withdraw to your castle on your oath. You can
promise not to go beyond your boundaries, and you will be
better off than here.

Götz: They will say my possessions are forfeit to the Emperor.

Sickingen: Then we will say you mean to live there and pay rent
until the Emperor confers them on you again in fief. Let them
squirm like eels in a basket, but they won't give us the slip.
They will talk about Imperial Majesty and about their commission. That will make no difference to us. I know the Em-

peror too, and count for something with him. He has always
wanted to have you in his army. You won't be at your castle
very long before you get called up.

GÖTZ: God make it soon, before I unlearn how to fight.

SICKINGEN: Courage is not unlearned any more than it is learned.
Don't worry about anything. Once your affairs are in order I
will go to court—for my enterprise is beginning to ripen. Favor-
able signs tell me: "Start!" All I have to do yet is to sound out
the Emperor's sentiments. Trier and the Palatine will be expecting the sky to collapse sooner than for me to descend upon
them. And I mean to descend like a hailstorm! And if we can
shape our destiny you will presently be the brother-in-law of
an Electoral Prince. I was counting on your fist in this enterprise.

GÖTZ *(looks at his hand.)*: O this was foreshadowed by the dream
I had when I promised Maria to Weislingen the following day.
He promised me loyalty and held so tight onto my right hand
that it came out of the vambrace as though it had been broken
off. Ah! I am more defenseless at this minute than I was when
it was shot off. Weislingen! Weislingen!

SICKINGEN: Forget the traitor. We will wipe out his schemes, un-
dermine his esteem, and conscience and shame shall eat him
to death. I see, in my mind I see my enemies and your enemies
overthrown. Götz, just a half a year more!

GÖTZ: Your soul soars aloft. I don't know, for some time now
no joyous prospects seem to want to open in mine.—I've been in
more trouble before this, I've been a prisoner once before, and
I have never felt the way I feel now.

SICKINGEN: Luck brings courage. Come on in to the curliwigs.
They've had their say long enough; let us assume the burden
for a change.

(Exeunt.)

*

[Scene 4]

Adelheid's castle.
Adelheid. Weislingen.

ADELHEID: That is odious!

WEISLINGEN: I clenched my teeth. Such a wonderful scheme, so
neatly executed, and then to let him go to his castle after all!
That damned Sickingen!

ADELHEID: They shouldn't have done it.

WEISLINGEN: They were caught. What could they do? Sickingen
threatened them with fire and sword, that overbearing, hot-
tempered man! I hate him. His prestige swells like a river that
swallowed up a couple of brooks—the others will follow of
themselves.

ADELHEID: Didn't they have an Emperor?

WEISLINGEN: My dear wife, he is only the shadow of one. He is
getting old and peevish. When he heard what had happened
and the other government councilors were getting excited, he
said: "Leave them alone. I can afford to allow old Götz that
little spot, and if he is quiet there, what do you have to com-
plain about in him?" We spoke of the welfare of the state.
"O!" said he. "If I only had advisors all along who would have
directed my uneasy mind more toward the happiness of in-
dividual human beings!"

ADELHEID: He is losing the spirit of a ruler.

WEISLINGEN: We went after Sickingen.—"He is my loyal servant."
said he, "and if he did not do it at my command, he neverthe-
less performed my will better than my authorized agents, and
I can call it good before or after the fact."

ADELHEID: It's enough to make one tear one's hair.

WEISLINGEN: All the same, I have not yet given up all hope. He
has been left in his castle on his knightly word to be quiet
there. That is impossible for him. We will soon have grounds
against him.

ADELHEID: And all the sooner because we can hope the Emperor will soon be leaving this world, and Charles, his admirable successor, shows promise of more majestic views.

WEISLINGEN: Charles? He has not yet been either elected or crowned.[1]

ADELHEID: Who doesn't wish and hope for it?

WEISLINGEN: You have a high opinion of his qualities. One would almost think you saw them with other eyes.

ADELHEID: You offend me, Weislingen. Do you know me to be such?

WEISLINGEN: I said nothing to offend you. But I cannot remain silent in the face of it. Charles's unusual attention toward you makes me uneasy.

ADELHEID: And my conduct?

WEISLINGEN: You are a woman. You women hate no one who pays court to you.

ADELHEID: While men. . . . ?

WEISLINGEN: It gnaws at my heart, this fearful thought. Adelheid!

ADELHEID: Can I cure your folly?

WEISLINGEN: If you wanted to! You could withdraw from court.

ADELHEID: Name ways and means. Aren't you at court? Am I supposed to leave you and my friends in order to entertain myself with owls at my castle? No, Weislingen, no good would come of that. Be reassured. You know how I love you.

WEISLINGEN: The sacred anchor in this storm, as long as the rope doesn't break.

(Exit.)

ADELHEID: So that's the way you're starting in! That's all I needed! The enterprises of my heart are too great for you to stand in their way. Charles! Great and excellent man, and Emperor be-

---

[1]Charles V, elected Holy Roman Emperor 1519, crowned 1520.

sides! And should he be the only one among men not to be flattered by the possession of my favor? Weislingen, don't dream of hindering me! Or else into the ground you go, for my path goes over you.

(Enter Franz with a letter.)

FRANZ: Here, my Lady.

ADELHEID: Did Charles himself give it to you?

FRANZ: Yes.

ADELHEID: What is the matter? You look so woebegone.

FRANZ: It is your will that I am to languish away and die. In the years of hope you make me despair.

ADELHEID: [*aside*]: I am sorry for him. And how little it costs me to make him happy!—Be of good spirits, lad. I feel your love and loyalty and I shall never be ungrateful.

FRANZ *(choked up)*: If you were capable of that I would surely perish. My God, I haven't a drop of blood in me that isn't yours, nor a thought except to love you and to do what pleases you.

ADELHEID: Dear boy!

FRANZ: You're humoring me. *(Bursting into tears)* If this devotion deserves nothing more than to see others preferred to me, to see all your thoughts directed toward this Charles. . . . .

ADELHEID: You don't know what you're asking, still less what you're saying.

FRANZ *(stamping his foot in vexation and anger)*: I don't want any more of it. I won't play the go-between any longer.

ADELHEID: Franz! You are forgetting yourself.

FRANZ: To sacrifice myself! My dear master!

ADELHEID: Leave my sight.

FRANZ: My Lady!

ADELHEID: Go, reveal my secret to your dear master. I was a fool to take you for something you aren't.

FRANZ: Dear, gracious Lady, you know I love you.

ADELHEID: And you used to be my friend, so close to my heart. Go, betray me.

FRANZ: I'd sooner tear my heart out of my body! Forgive me, my Lady. My heart is too full, my senses cannot endure it.

ADELHEID: Dear, warm-hearted youth!

(She takes his hands, draws him to her, and their kisses meet.

He falls upon her neck weeping.)

Leave me!

FRANZ *(choked with tears at her neck)*: My God! My God!

ADELHEID: Leave me. The walls are traitors. Leave me! *(She disengages herself.)* Do not waver in your love and loyalty, and the most beautiful reward will be yours.

(Exit.)

FRANZ: The most beautiful reward! Just let me live till then! I would murder my father if he contested this place with me!

*

[SCENE 5]

Jaxthausen.

Götz at a table. Elizabeth with her work beside him. A lamp and writing materials are on the table.

GÖTZ: I just can't get the taste for idleness and my restriction becomes more oppressive every day. I wish I could sleep, or just be able to pretend that quiet is something pleasant.

ELIZABETH: Then go on writing your biography that you have started. Put into the hands of your friends a testimonial to shame your enemies. Provide a noble posterity with the joy of not misunderstanding you.

GÖTZ: Oh! Writing is busy idleness, I find it sour. While I am writing about what I have done, I am annoyed at the loss of the time in which I could be doing something.

ELIZABETH (*takes the written pages.*) : Don't be foolish. You are up to your first imprisonment at Heilbronn.

GÖTZ: That was always an unlucky place for me.

ELIZABETH (*reads*) : "In that place there were several members of the League who told me I had been foolish to confront my worst enemies when I could have guessed they would not deal forbearingly with me. Then I answered: . . ."— Well, what did you answer? Go on and write it.

GÖTZ: I said: "If I risk my skin for others' property and money, shan't I risk it for my word?"

ELIZABETH: You have that reputation.

GÖTZ: And they're not going to take it away from me! They've taken everything else, property, liberty, . . .

ELIZABETH: That was at the time when I encountered the lords of Miltenberg and Singlingen at the inn and they didn't know me. Then I had a pleasure as if I had borne a son. They were praising you among themselves and saying: "He is the model of a knight, brave and noble in his liberty and calm and loyal in misfortune."

GÖTZ: Let them show me one man to whom I have broken my word! And God knows that I have sweated harder to serve my neighbor than myself and that I have worked for the name of a brave and loyal knight and not to gain lofty riches and rank. And, thanks be to God, what I strove for has been granted me.

(*Enter Lerse and Georg with game.*)

Greetings to you, gallant huntsmen!

GEORG: From gallant horsemen that is what we have turned into. Boots are easily converted into slippers.

LERSE: Hunting is still something, and a kind of warfare.

GEORG: If only we didn't always have to be having something to do with Imperials around here! You remember, Sir, how you prophesied that if the world turned upside down we would become hunters? Here we are, without that.

GÖTZ: It amounts to the same thing, we are moved out of our sphere.

GEORG: These are critical times. For a week now there's been a fearful comet visible, and all Germany is in terror that it may mean the death of the Emperor, who is very ill.

GÖTZ: Very ill! Our road is coming to an end.

LERSE: And here in the vicinity there are still more frightful changes. The peasants have started a horrible rebellion.[1]

GÖTZ: Where?

LERSE: In the heart of Swabia. They're scorching the land and burning and murdering. I'm afraid they'll lay the entire province waste.

GEORG: There's a terrible war. Some hundred villages are already in revolt, and more every day. Recently a storm wind uprooted whole forests, and shortly after that, in the district where the rebellion began, two fiery swords were seen crosswise in the air.

GÖTZ: Then some of my good knights and friends must surely be suffering innocently along with others.

GEORG: A shame we are not allowed to ride out to war!

---

[1]Emperor Maximilian died January 12, 1519. The Peasants War occurred in 1525.

ACT V

[SCENE 1]

The Peasants War. Tumult and pillaging in a village. Women and old men with children and packs, in flight.

AN OLD MAN: Get along, get along, so we escape from these murdering curs!

A WOMAN: Merciful God! How blood-red the sky is! The setting sun is blood-red!

A MOTHER: That means a fire.

THE WOMAN: My husband! My husband!

THE OLD MAN: Get along! Get along! Into the woods!

(They move on.)

LINK: Whoever resists, mow him down! The town is ours. See that none of the harvest is destroyed and none of it gets left here. Plunder everything and fast! We're going to set fire right away.

METZLER (*running down the hill*): How're things going with you, Link?[1]

LINK: Topsy-turvily, as you see. You're here for the clean-out. Where from?

METZLER: From Weinsberg. *There* was a party!

LINK: How so?

METZLER: We mowed them down so it was a joy to see.

LINK: Who all?

METZLER: Dietrich von Weiler led the dance.[2] The money! There

---

[1] Jörg Metzler, identical with the character in Act I, Scene 1, was an actual historical personage, as was "Link," nickname of Hannes Bermetter.

[2] The last dance was called a "clean-out" (*Kehraus*).

we were in full pack howling like mad all around, and he was up there on the church tower wanting to deal with us nice-like. Bang! Somebody shot him through the head. Up we streaked like lightning, and out through the window came the fellow.

LINK: Ah!

METZLER *(to the peasants)*: Shall I put legs on you, you curs? The way they dawdle and hang back, the donkeys!

LINK: Set fire! Let's roast 'em inside! Come on! Go to it, you rascals!

METZLER: Then we led out Helfenstein, and Eltershofen, around thirteen of them nobles, eighty all told. Led them out on the plain toward Heilbronn. And then there was a jubilating and a tumult-making from our lads as that long line of poor wealthy sinners came along, gawking at each other, gawking at the ground and the sky! Before they knew it they were surrounded and mowed down with pikes, all of them.

LINK: And I had to miss that!

METZLER: Never had so much fun in all my born days.

LINK *(to a peasant)*: Get a move on! Out with you!

THE PEASANT: Everything is empty.

LINK: Then set fire at every corner.

METZLER: It'll make a cute little fire. D'you see how those fellows tumbled all over each other and squeaked like frogs! My heart ran over like a glass of brandy. There was a Rixinger there. When that fellow used to ride to the hunt with his plume on his hat and his nostrils wide, the way he would drive us on ahead of him with the dogs and like the dogs. I hadn't seen him since then, but I caught his monkey-face right away. Bash! and the pike was between his ribs, and there he lay and stretched out all fours across his companions. Those fellows went twitching down on top of each other like rabbits when the dogs run them down.

LINK: It's smoking nice already.

METZLER: It's burning over in back there. Let's amble down with the booty to the main force.

LINK: Where's it camped?

METZLER: This side of Heilbronn. They're hard up for a leader that all the people would have respect for; for *we*'re only their own sort, after all. They feel it and they're getting hard to handle.

LINK: Who're they thinking of?

METZLER: Max Stumpf or Götz von Berlichingen.

LINK: That'd be good. It'd give the thing a polish if Götz took it on; he's always passed for an upright knight. Come on! Come on! We're heading for Heilbronn. Pass the word along!

METZLER: The fire'll light our way for a good stretch. Have you seen the big comet?

LINK: Yes. That's a hideous, dreadful sign! If we march all night we'll see it all right. It rises around one.

METZLER: And stays only five quarters of an hour. It looks like a bended arm with a sword, kind of blood-yellow.

LINK: Have you seen the three stars at the tip and sides of the sword?

METZLER: And that broad cloud-colored tail with thousands and thousands of streamers like pikes, and in between like little swords.

LINK: I shuddered to look at it. The way it was all so pale red, and all those fiery bright flames around, and in between those cruel faces with shaggy heads and beards!

METZLER: Did you see them too? And the way it all keeps flashing higgeldy-piggeldy, as if it were lying in a gory sea and fermenting inside, till it makes your senses swim?

LINK: Come on! Come on!

(Exeunt.)

*

[SCENE 2]

A field. In the distance two villages and a cloister
are seen burning.
Kohl. Wild. Max Stumpf. Bands of soldiery.

MAX STUMPF: You can't want me to be your leader. It wouldn't
be any good for you or for me. I'm a Palatine subject, so how
should I lead men against my master? You would always think
I didn't have my heart in it.

KOHL: We knew you'd find an excuse.

(Enter Götz, Lerse, and Georg.)

GÖTZ: What do you want of me?

KOHL: You're going to be our leader.

GÖTZ: Am I supposed to break my knightly word to the Emperor
and leave my district?

WILD: That's no excuse.

GÖTZ: Even if I were completely free, and you meant to go on
acting the way you did at Weinsberg with the nobles and gentry
and to keep carrying on this way, with the country all around
burning and bleeding, and I am supposed to help you in your
shameful, crazy doings—you'll have to kill me first like a mad
dog before I would be your head!

KOHL: If that hadn't happened, maybe it never would happen.

STUMPF: That was just the trouble, they didn't have a leader they
respected, one that could put a stop to their madness. Assume
this command, I beg you, Götz! The princes will be grateful
to you, all Germany will. It will be for the best interests of
everybody. Human beings and provinces will be spared.

GÖTZ: Why don't you take it over?

STUMPF: I've said I'd have no part of it.

KOHL: We don't have time for dillydallying and long pointless
speeches. Short and sweet: Götz, be our leader or else look out

for your castle and your skin. Two hours' time to think it over.
Put a guard on him.

GÖTZ: What's the good of that? I've got my mind made up as
much now as later. Why did you start out on this expedition?
To get back your rights and liberties? Why are you raging so
and laying the land waste? If you are willing to cut out all
these misdoings and act like proper people that know what
they want, I'm willing to help you get your demands and be
your leader for one week.

WILD: What happened, happened in the first flush, and it doesn't
need you to hinder us in the future.

KOHL: You have to agree to it for a quarter of a year at least.

STUMPF: Make it four weeks. Then you will both be satisfied.

GÖTZ: All right.

KOHL: Your hand!

GÖTZ: And swear to me to send out this contract you have made
with me in writing to all bands, and to live up to it strictly
under penalty.

WILD: All right! We'll do that!

GÖTZ: So I contract myself to you for four weeks.

STUMPF: Good luck! Whatever you do, spare our gracious master,
the Count Palatine.

KOHL *(softly)*: Watch him. See that no one talks to him outside
your presence.

GÖTZ: Lerse! Go to my wife. Stand by her. She will have news of
me soon.

*(Exeunt Götz, Stumpf, Georg, Lerse,
and several peasants.)*
(Enter Metzler and Link.)

METZLER: What's this we hear about a contract? Why a contract?

LINK: It's a disgrace, entering into a contract like that.

KOHL: We know what we're doing as well as you do, and we're
free agents.

WILD: This raging around and burning and murdering had to stop some time, tomorrow if not today. This way we've got ourselves a brave leader besides.

METZLER: What's this about stopping! You traitor! What are we here for? To take revenge on our enemies and help ourselves up!—Some princely lackey put this into your head.

KOHL: Come on, Wild, he's like an ox.

(Exeunt.)

METZLER: Go on! There won't a band stick with you. The rascals! Link, let's stir up the others to go and set fire to Miltenberg over yonder, and if there's any to-do on account of the contract, we'll knock all the contractors' heads off.

LINK: We've still got the bulk of the band on our side.

*

[SCENE 3]

A hill and a valley. A mill at the valley's bottom.
A troop of horsemen. Weislingen comes out of the mill
with Franz and a messenger.

WEISLINGEN: My horse!—You told the other gentlemen too?

THE MESSENGER: At least seven companies will join you in the forest behind Miltenberg. The peasants are moving around down there. Messengers have been sent everywhere, the whole League will soon be gathered. It can't fail. They say there's dissension among them.

WEISLINGEN: All the better.—Franz!

FRANZ: Sir?

WEISLINGEN: Carry out the instructions exactly. I lay the charge to your soul. Give her the letter. She is to leave the court and go to my castle. At once! You are to watch her ride away and then report to me.

FRANZ: It shall be done as you command.

WEISLINGEN: Tell her she *has to* want to!

(to the messenger)

Lead us by the shortest and best road.

THE MESSENGER: We have to go around. All the streams are in flood from the terrible rains.

*

[SCENE 4]

Jaxthausen.
Elizabeth. Lerse.

LERSE: Take comfort, my Lady!

ELIZABETH: Oh, Lerse, he had tears in his eyes as he took farewell of me. It is cruel, cruel!

LERSE: He will come back.

ELIZABETH: That isn't it. When he used to ride out to seek honorable victory there was no pain around my heart. I used to look forward to his return, which I am now uneasy about.

LERSE: Such a noble man. . . .

ELIZABETH: Do not call him that, it starts my sorrows afresh. The scoundrels! They threatened to murder him and set fire to his castle.—When he does come back—I will see him grim, grim. His enemies will fix up lying articles of accusation, and he will not be able to say "No!"

LERSE: He can and will.

ELIZABETH: He has left his assigned district. Say "No" to that!

LERSE: No! He was forced to it. Where are the grounds for condemning him?

ELIZABETH: Malice doesn't look for grounds, only excuses. He has joined up with rebels, evil-doers, murderers, he has marched at their head. Say "No" to that!

LERSE: Stop tormenting yourself and me. Didn't they solemnly promise him not to perpetrate any more actions like the ones at Weinsberg? Didn't I hear them myself saying half in remorse: "If it hadn't happened, perhaps it never would happen?" Wouldn't the princes and lords have to be grateful to him if he voluntarily became the leader of an unruly mob in order to put a stop to their madness and spare so many people and pieces of property?

ELIZABETH: You are a winning advocate.—If they took him prisoner and treated him as a rebel and misused his grey head. . . . Lerse, I would lose my mind.

LERSE: Grant her body sleep, dear Father of mankind, if Thou wilt not grant comfort to her soul!

ELIZABETH: Georg promised to bring word. But he won't be allowed either to do as he wishes. They are worse than prisoners. I know they are guarding them like enemies. Good Georg! He would not leave his master.

LERSE: My heart bled when he sent me away. If *you* had not needed my help, not all the perils of a shameful death could have parted me from him.

ELIZABETH: I don't know where Sickingen is. If I could only send Maria a messenger!

LERSE: Just write, and I will see to it.

(Exeunt.)

*

[SCENE 5]

Near a village.
Götz. Georg.

GÖTZ: Quick, to horse, Georg! I see Miltenberg burning. So that's the way they keep a contract! Ride over and let them know my mind. The murderous arsonists! I resign from them. Let them make some gypsy their leader, not me. Quick, Georg!

(Exit Georg.)

I wish I were a thousand miles away in the deepest dungeon there is in Turkey! If I could only get away from them with honor! I drum it into them every day, I tell them the bitterest truths, so they will get tired of me and let me go.

(Enter a stranger.)

THE STRANGER: God's greeting to you, very noble Sir!

GÖTZ: God reward you! What do you bring? Your name?

THE STRANGER: That is not to the point. I come to tell you your head is in danger. The leaders are tired of taking such harsh words from you and they have decided to put you out of the way. Keep your temper or else look to your escape, and God be your guide!

(Exit.)

GÖTZ: To take leave of your life this way, Götz, to end like this! So be it! Then my death will be the surest sign to the world that I have nothing in common with these curs.

(Enter several peasants.)

THE FIRST PEASANT: Sir! Sir! They're beaten, they're taken prisoner!

GÖTZ: Who?

THE SECOND PEASANT: The ones that burned Miltenberg. A troop of Leaguists moved out from behind the hill and attacked them all of a sudden.

GÖTZ: Their reward awaits them.—O Georg! Georg!—They've captured him along with the scoundrels. . . . My Georg! My Georg. . . . !

(Enter the leaders.)

LINK: Up, Captain, up. There's no time to lose. The enemy is near by and in force.

GÖTZ: Who set fire to Miltenberg?

METZLER: If you want to make a fuss, we'll show you how no fuss is made.

KOHL: Look to your hide and ours. Come on! Come on!

GÖTZ (*to Metzler*): Are you threatening me? You good-for-nothing! Do you think you're more frightening to me because the Count of Helfenstein's blood is clotted on your clothes?

METZLER: Berlichingen!

GÖTZ: You can mention my name and my children will not be ashamed of it!

METZLER: You coward! Prince's lackey!

*(Götz hits him over the head so he falls.
The others intervene.)*

KOHL: You're insane. The enemy is breaking through on all sides, and you are feuding!

LINK: Come on! Come on!

(Battle and tumult.)
(Enter Weislingen and horsemen.)

WEISLINGEN: After them! After them! They're fleeing! Don't let rain and darkness keep you from them. Götz is among them, I hear. Put your hearts into it so you catch him. He's badly wounded, our men report.

(Exeunt the horsemen.)

And once I get you. . . . !—It will still be mercy if we execute you secretly in prison.—Then his light will go out in the memory of men, and you can breathe more freely, foolish heart.

(Exit.)

*

[SCENE 6]

Night in the wild forest. A gypsy encampment.
A gypsywoman by the fire.

THE GYPSYWOMAN: Mend the thatch over the cave-door, daughter. There'll be rain a-plenty tonight.

(Enter a boy.)

THE BOY: A hamster, mother. There! Two field mice.

THE MOTHER: I'll skin them and roast them for you, and you shall have a cap from the pelts.—You're bleeding?

THE BOY: Hamster bit me.

THE MOTHER: Fetch me kindling to make the fire burn up. When your father comes he'll be wet through and through.

(Enter another gypsywoman with a child on her back.)

THE FIRST WOMAN: Did you make a good haul?

THE SECOND WOMAN: Little enough. The district is full of tumult all around so no one's life is safe. Two villages are blazing.

THE FIRST WOMAN: Is that a fire yonder, that glow? I've been looking at it for a long time. We've got so used to fiery signs in the sky lately.

(Enter the gypsy leader and three companions.)

THE LEADER: Do you hear the Wild Huntsman?[1]

THE FIRST WOMAN: He's passing right over us.

THE LEADER: How the dogs do bark! Bow! Wow!

THE SECOND GYPSY: The whips crack.

THIRD GYPSY: The huntsmen are shouting Holla Ho!

THE MOTHER: Well, you have brought in the devil's pack!

THE LEADER: We fished in troubled waters. The peasants themselves are plundering, so we may as well.

SECOND WOMAN: What have you got there, Wolf?

---

[1]The Wild Huntsman with his fellow-huntsmen and dogs is a folklore personification of the tempest. (Originally he was the god Wotan himself.)

WOLF: A rabbit—there—and a rooster, a roasting spit, a bundle of laundry, three cooking spoons, and a horse bridle.

STICKS: I've got a woolen blanket, a pair of boots, and tinder and powder.

THE MOTHER: All soaking wet. Let's dry it out, give it here.

THE LEADER: Hark, a horse! Go, see what it is.

(Enter Götz on horseback.)

GÖTZ: Thank God! Yonder I see a fire. They're gypsies. My wounds are gushing blood, the enemy is after me. Great God, Thou dost make a vile end of me!

THE LEADER: Is it peacefully you come?

GÖTZ: I implore you for help. My wounds have made me weak. Help me from my horse!

THE LEADER: Help him! A noble man in looks and speech.

WOLF *(softly)*: It's Götz von Berlichingen!

THE LEADER: Welcome! Everything we have is yours.

GÖTZ: I thank you.

THE LEADER: Come into my tent.

*

[SCENE 7]

The leader's tent.
The leader. Götz.

THE LEADER: Call Mother and have her bring blood-root and a plaster.

(Götz takes off his armor.)

Here is my Sunday jerkin.

GÖTZ: God reward you.

(The mother binds up his wounds.)

THE LEADER: It warms my heart to have you here.

GÖTZ: You know me?

THE LEADER: Who wouldn't know you! Götz, we'd give our lives and blood for you.

(Enter Schricks.)

SCHRICKS: Horsemen coming through the woods. They're Leaguists.

THE LEADER: Your pursuers! They shan't get to you. Come on, Schricks! Let the others know. We know the trails better than they do and we'll shoot them down before they sight us.

GÖTZ *(alone)*: O my Emperor, my Emperor! Robbers shield your children.

(A sharp exchange of firing is heard.)

Those wild lads, tough and true!

(Enter a gypsywoman.)

THE GYPSYWOMAN: Make your escape! The enemy is getting the upper hand.

GÖTZ: Where is my horse?

THE GYPSYWOMAN: Near by.

GÖTZ *(belts on his sword and mounts without armor.)*: For the last time they shall feel my arm. I'm not that weak yet.

(Exit.)

THE GYPSYWOMAN: He's galloping to our men.

(Flight.)

WOLF: Away! Away! All is lost. Our leader's shot. Götz is captured.

(Howling of women and flight.)

*

[SCENE 8]

Adelheid's bedchamber.
Adelheid with a letter.

ADELHEID: He or I! What insolence! To threaten me!—We shall

anticipate you. What is that stealthy movement across the outer room?

(A knock.)

Who is out there?

FRANZ *(softly)*: Open the door, my Lady.

ADELHEID: Franz! He deserves to have me open the door.

(She lets him in.)

FRANZ *(falls on her neck)*: My dear Lady!

ADELHEID: Impudent! What if someone had heard you!

FRANZ: Oh, everybody is asleep, everybody!

ADELHEID: What do you want?

FRANZ: It gives me no rest. My lord's threats, your fate, my heart!

ADELHEID: He was very angry as you took leave of him?

FRANZ: As I had never seen him before. To her estates she shall go, he said; she *has to* want to!

ADELHEID: And we obey?

FRANZ: I don't know, my Lady.

ADELHEID: Foolish, betrayed youth, you don't see where this is leading. Here he knows I am safe. For he has long had designs on my freedom. He wants me on his estates. There he has the power to treat me as his hatred bids.

FRANZ: He shall not!

ADELHEID: Will you prevent him?

FRANZ: He shall not!

ADELHEID: I foresee my total misery. He will take me out of his castle by force and lock me up in a convent.

FRANZ: Hell and death!

ADELHEID: Will you rescue me?

FRANZ: Anything, anything but that!

ADELHEID *(in tears, embracing him)*: Franz, oh! to make our escape!

FRANZ: Down he shall go, I'll plant my foot on his neck.

ADELHEID: No temper! You shall have a letter to him, full of humility, saying that I obey him. And pour this little phial into his drink.

FRANZ: Let me have it! You shall be free!

ADELHEID: Free! When you will no longer come stealing to me on tiptoe and trembling . . . when I shall no more say anxiously to you: Go, Franz, the morning is near.

*

[SCENE 9]

Heilbronn, in front of the prison.
Elizabeth. Lerse.

LERSE: God lift your misery from you, my Lady! Maria is here.

ELIZABETH: Thanks be to God! Lerse, we are sunk into ghastly misery. Now it is all just as I foresensed. Captured, thrown into the deepest dungeon as a rebel and miscreant . . .

LERSE: I know all about it.

ELIZABETH: You know nothing, nothing. The grief is too great! His age, his wounds, a creeping fever, and more than all of that, the gloom of his soul to think it should end this way with him!

LERSE: Yes, and then to have Weislingen as the commissioner.

ELIZABETH: Weislingen?

LERSE: They have proceeded to unheard-of executions. Metzler was burned alive, hundreds broken on the wheel, impaled on pikes, beheaded, drawn and quartered. The countryside around looks like a shambles where human flesh is cheap.

ELIZABETH: Weislingen the commissioner! My God! A ray of hope. I'll have Maria go to him, he cannot refuse her anything. He always had a soft heart, and if he sees her whom

he loved so much, who was made so unhappy because of him.
. . . Where is she?

LERSE: Still at the inn.

ELIZABETH: Take me to her. She must start right away. I fear the
worst.

*

[SCENE 10]

Weislingen's castle.

WEISLINGEN: I am so sick, so weak. All my bones are hollow. A
miserable fever has eaten out the marrow. No rest or repose,
day or night. Poisonous dreams amid half-sleep. Last night I
met Götz in the forest. He drew his sword and challenged me.
I reached for mine and my hand failed me. Then he thrust it
into his sheath, looked at me contemptuously, and followed
me.—He is a prisoner, and I tremble before him. Wretched
man! Your word has condemned him to death, and you cower
like a miscreant before his dream-phantom! —And is he to die?
—Götz! Götz!—We human beings do not steer our own courses;
power over us is given to evil spirits to work their hellish mis-
chief to our destruction.

(*He sits down.*)

Feeble! Feeble! How blue my fingernails are! — A cold, cold,
consuming sweat paralyses my every limb. Everything spins
before my eyes. If I could only sleep! Oh. . .

(*Enter Maria.*)

Jesus and Mary!—Leave me in peace! Leave me in peace!—
That shape is all I needed! She is dying, Maria, she is dying
and she is appearing to me.—Leave me, blessed spirit! I am
miserable enough.

MARIA: Weislingen, I am not a ghost. I am Maria.

WEISLINGEN: That is her voice.

MARIA: I have come to beg you for my brother's life. He is innocent, no matter how much he seems to blame.

WEISLINGEN: Be still, Maria! You angel of heaven, you bring with you the torments of hell. Do not speak any more!

MARIA: And is my brother to die? Weislingen, it is monstrous that I should have to tell you he is innocent, that I have to show my grief in order to keep you from this horrible murder. Your soul is possessed to its uttermost depth by hostile Powers. And this is Adelbert!

WEISLINGEN: You see that the consuming breath of death has breathed upon me, my strength is sinking toward the grave. I would be dying as one in misery, and you come to plunge me into despair. If I could only speak, your utmost hatred would melt away to pity and sorrow. O Maria! Maria!

MARIA: Weislingen, my brother is wasting away in prison. His grievous wounds, his age! And if you were capable of harming his grey head . . . Weislingen, we would despair.

WEISLINGEN: Enough.

(*He pulls the bell-cord. Enter Franz in extreme agitation.*)

FRANZ: Sir?

WEISLINGEN: Those papers there, Franz!

(*Franz fetches them. Weislingen tears open a packet
and shows Maria a paper.*)

Here is your brother's death warrant, signed.

MARIA: God in heaven!

WEISLINGEN: Here: I tear it up. He lives. But can I recreate what I have destroyed? Don't weep so, Franz! Good youth, your misery touches my heart deeply.

(*Franz throws himself down before him
and embraces his knees.*)

MARIA (*to herself*) : He is very ill. The sight of him rends my heart. How I loved him once! And coming near him now, I realize how deeply.

WEISLINGEN: Get up, Franz, and stop your weeping. I can get well again. Hope is with the living.

FRANZ: You will not. You must die.

WEISLINGEN: I must?

FRANZ (*beside himself*) : Poisoned! Poisoned! By your wife! —I! I!

(*He rushes away.*)

WEISLINGEN: Maria, follow him! He is in despair!

(*Exit Maria.*)

Poisoned by my wife! Oh! Oh! I can feel it! Torment and death!

MARIA (*offstage*) : Help! Help!

WEISLINGEN (*tries to get up.*) : My God! I can't!

(*Reenter Maria.*)

MARIA: He is dead. He threw himself in a frenzy out of the window of the great hall into the Main.

WEISLINGEN: He is well off.—Your brother is out of danger. The other commissioners, Seckendorf especially, are his friends. They will allow him knightly imprisonment on the pledge of his word. Farewell, Maria, and go.

MARIA: I will stay with you, poor forsaken man.

WEISLINGEN: Forsaken and poor indeed! Thou art a dread avenger, God!—My wife . . .

MARIA: Give up these thoughts. Turn your heart to the All Merciful.

WEISLINGEN: Go, dear soul, leave me to my misery.—Monstrous! Even your presence, Maria, the last consolation, is torment.

MARIA (*to herself*) : Give me strength, O God! My soul succumbs with his.

WEISLINGEN: Alas! Alas! Poisoned by my wife!—My Franz cor-
rupted by the vile woman! How she waits, listens for the messenger to bring the news: "He is dead." And you, Maria!
Maria! Why did you come to weaken the sleeping memory of
my sins! Leave me! Leave me, so I can die!

MARIA: Let me stay. You are alone. Imagine I am your nurse.
Forget everything. May God forget everything about you as I
forget everything about you!

WEISLINGEN: Soul full of love, pray for me, pray for me! My
heart is shut.

MARIA: He will have mercy on you.—You are weak.

WEISLINGEN: I am dying, I am dying, and I can't die. And in
this fearful struggle between life and death there are the torments of hell.

MARIA: Have mercy on him, have mercy on him! Cast just one
glance of Thy love upon his heart so it may be opened to comfort and so his spirit may bring hope, the hope of life, into
death!

*

[SCENE 11]

In a dismal, narrow, vaulted chamber.
The judges of the secret tribunal, all masked.[1]

THE ELDEST: Judges of the secret tribunal, swear by noose and
by sword to be blameless, to judge in secrecy, to punish in secrecy like God! If your hearts and your hands are pure, then
raise up your arms and over the wrongdoers cry out: Woe!
Woe!

ALL: Woe! Woe!

---

[1]The historical secret tribunal (*Fehmgericht* or *Vehmgericht*) of the middle ages always met in the open air and by daylight, its members wore no
masks, and women were not usually subject to its jurisdiction.

THE ELDEST: Summoner, begin the session.

THE SUMMONER: I the Summoner summon accusation against the wrongdoer. Whatever man whose heart is pure, whose hands are pure to swear by noose and by sword, let him accuse by noose and by sword, accuse, accuse!

THE ACCUSER (*steps up.*) : My heart is pure of wrongdoing, my hands of innocent blood. May God forgive me evil thoughts and hinder the way of the will! I raise my hand aloft and I accuse, accuse, accuse!

THE ELDEST: Whom do you accuse?

THE ACCUSER: I accuse by noose and by sword Adelheid von Weislingen. She has committed adultery and poisoned her husband through her page. The page has condemned himself; the husband is dead.

THE ELDEST: Do you swear to the God of Truth that you accuse in truth?

THE ACCUSER: I swear.

THE ELDEST: If it is found false, do you offer your neck to the penalty of murder and of adultery?

THE ACCUSER: I so offer.

THE ELDEST: Your voices.

(*They speak secretly with him.*)

THE ACCUSER: Judges of the secret tribunal, what is your judgment on Adelheid von Weislingen who is charged with adultery and murder?

THE ELDEST: She shall die, die the bitter double death, and by rope and by dagger doubly atone for the double wrongdoing! Raise your hands aloft and cry woe upon her! Woe! Woe! into the hands of the Avenger!

ALL: Woe! Woe! Woe!

THE ELDEST: Avenger, Avenger, step forth!

(*The Avenger steps forth.*)

Take here this rope and this sword wherewith to exterminate her from the sight of Heaven within one week's time. Wheresoever you find her, down with her to the dust!—You judges who judge in secret and who punish in secret like God, keep your hearts from wrongdoing and your hands from innocent blood.

*

[Scene 12]

The courtyard of an inn.
Maria. Lerse.

MARIA: The horses have rested enough. Let us go, Lerse.
LERSE: Rest rather till morning. The night is far too unfriendly.
MARIA: Lerse, I can have no rest until I have seen my brother. Let us go. The weather is clearing; we can expect a fine day.
LERSE: As you command.

*

[Scene 13]

Heilbronn, in the prison.
Götz. Elizabeth.

ELIZABETH: Speak to me, dear husband, I beg you. Your silence troubles me. You are consumed with inner fire. Come, let us look to your wounds; they are much improved. I do not recognize you any longer in this despondent gloom.
GÖTZ: Were you looking for Götz? He is long since gone. Little by little they have maimed me—my hand, my freedom, my property, and my good name. My head, what is that worth?— What do you hear of Georg? Has Lerse gone for Georg?

ELIZABETH: Yes, my dear. Be of good cheer. Many things can change.

GÖTZ: Whom God strikes down does not rise again. I know best what lies upon my shoulders. Misfortune I am accustomed to endure. And now it's not Weislingen alone, not just the peasants alone, not the Emperor's death and my wounds—it is all these together. My hour has come. I had hoped it would be like my life. *His* will be done!

ELIZABETH: Will you not eat something?

GÖTZ: Nothing, wife. Look how the sun is shining outside.

ELIZABETH: A beautiful spring day.

GÖTZ: I wonder, my dear, whether you could persuade the jailer to let me out for half an hour in his little garden, so that I could enjoy the lovely sunlight and the clear sky and the pure air?

ELIZABETH: Right away, and he will surely do it.

*

[SCENE 14]

The little garden adjoining the prison.
Maria. Lerse.

MARIA: Go in and see how things stand.

(Exit Lerse.)
(Enter Elizabeth and the jailer.)

ELIZABETH: God reward you for your love and loyalty to my word.

(Exit the jailer.)

Maria, what do you bring?

MARIA: My brother's safety. But, oh, my heart is torn. Weislingen is dead, poisoned by his wife. My husband is in danger.

The princes are getting too powerful for him. They say he is hemmed in and under siege.

ELIZABETH: Do not believe the rumor. And don't let Götz notice anything.

MARIA: How do things stand with him?

ELIZABETH: I was afraid he would not live to see your return. The hand of the Lord lies heavy upon him. And Georg is dead.

MARIA: Georg, the golden youth!

ELIZABETH: When those good-for-nothing rascals were burning Miltenberg, his master sent him to make them stop. Just then a troop of Leaguists attacked them.—Georg! If they had all acted as he did, they could not fail to have a good conscience. Many were cut down and Georg among them; he died a trooper's death.

MARIA: Does Götz know of it?

ELIZABETH: We are keeping it from him. He asks me ten times a day and ten times a day he sends me to find out what Georg is doing. I am afraid to deal that last thrust to his heart.

MARIA: O Lord, what are the hopes of this earth!

(*Enter Götz, Lerse, and the jailer.*)

GÖTZ: Almighty God! How good a man feels beneath Thy sky! How *free!*—The trees are putting out their buds and the whole world hopes. Farewell, my dear ones! My roots are cut away, my strength is sinking toward the grave.

ELIZABETH: Shall I send Lerse to the monastery to fetch your son so you can see him again and give him your blessing?

GÖTZ: Let him be, he is holier than I am, he does not need my blessing.—On our wedding day, Elizabeth, I didn't think I would die *this* way.—My old father gave us his blessing, and from his prayer welled forth a posterity of brave and noble sons.—Thou didst not hear him, and I am the last one.—Lerse, your face delights me more in the hour of death than in the bravest fight. Then my spirit guided yours; now you support me. Oh, if I could only see Georg once again and warm myself by his glance!—You cast down your eyes and weep . . . He is dead . . . Georg is dead . . . Then die, Götz!—You have outlived yourself, outlived the noble ones.—How did he die?—Oh, did they catch him among those murderous incendiaries, and has he been executed?

ELIZABETH: No, he was cut down at Miltenberg. He fought like a lion for his liberty.

GÖTZ: Thanks be to God!—He was the best lad under the sun, and brave.—Release my soul now!—Poor wife, I leave you in a vicious world. Lerse, do not forsake her!—Lock up your hearts more carefully than your doors. The times of Betrayal are coming, and to him free rein is given. The base will rule by cunning, and the noble man will fall into their snares. Maria, God give you back your husband again. May he not fall as low as he has climbed aloft. Selbitz is dead, and the good Emperor, and my Georg. Give me a drink of water.—Heavenly air . . . Freedom! Freedom!

(He dies.)

ELIZABETH: Only on high, on high with Thee. The world is a prison.

MARIA: Noble man! Noble man! Woe to the age that rejected you!

LERSE: Woe to the posterity that fails to appreciate you!